Social

Media

Marketing

Unveiling the Digital Marketing Landscape

(The Top Chatgpt Prompts for Viral Social Media Marketing Strategies)

John Greeson

Published By **Elena Holly**

John Greeson

All Rights Reserved

Social Media Marketing: Unveiling the Digital Marketing Landscape (The Top Chatgpt Prompts for Viral Social Media Marketing Strategies)

ISBN   978-1-7774719-7-2

No part of this guidebook shall be reproduced in any form without permission in writing from the publisher except in the case of brief quotations embodied in critical articles or reviews.

Legal & Disclaimer

The information contained in this book is not designed to replace or take the place of any form of medicine or professional medical advice. The information in this book has been provided for educational & entertainment purposes only.

The information contained in this book has been compiled from sources deemed reliable, and it is accurate to the best of the Author's knowledge; however, the Author cannot guarantee its accuracy and validity and cannot be held liable for any errors or omissions. Changes are periodically made to this book. You must consult your doctor or get professional medical advice before using any of the suggested remedies, techniques, or information in this book.

Table Of Contents

Chapter 1: What Is Smma?

This chapter will explore the fundamental notions and terminology pertaining SMMA SMMA (Social Media Marketing Agency) as well as SAAS (Software as the service) in this section. Anyone who is considering starting the SMMA journey should first be aware of the meanings of these concepts.

An organization called SMMA (or Social Media Marketing Agency, offers marketing and advertising services to its customers through different channels of social media. The services offered may comprise the management of communities, creation of content as well as management of accounts on social media marketing campaign design and execution, and much more. Because of the increasing importance of social media within the marketing strategy of businesses, SMMA has grown in popular recently.

Software as a Service in contrast it is also known as SAAS. This refers to a licensing and delivery system that allows the software to be accessible online and then hosted on the cloud. Most often, subscription-based SAAS applications offer users the ability to access software, without having to worry about installing or maintaining. In order to automate the tasks that are in the framework within the framework of SMMA, SAAS tools can help tremendously.

It is essential to understand other terms and ideas when you study the world of SMMA. They could include:

Digital Marketing Digital Marketing is the umbrella term used to describe a range of different marketing methods and methods that are used internet-based platforms like the internet, social networks email, web sites, and much more.

Target Audience: the specific audience or client base that you want to reach through your marketing efforts. Successful marketing campaigns need an accurate grasp of the target audience.

Niche Market: A niche market is specific segment of the market which focuses on a specific sector of product or customer. The chances of being successful increase when you choose the right niche, which allows you to concentrate your products as well as marketing efforts towards specific clients.

Branding: This is the act of creating your business an identifiable and identifiable brand image. The creation of your brand's identity and values, as well as visual elements (such such as logos and color schemes) and a style of communication is essential.

Lead Generation refers to the method of generating interest for your products and services from prospective clients. It can involve a range different strategies, like Lead capture forms social media ads and content marketing.

The best way to establish a strong basis for understanding and implementing efficient SMMA strategies and methods by becoming acquainted with the terms and concepts.

Building Your Brand

The success of running a SMMA (Social Media Marketing Agency) needs a strong branding. This chapter will explore the key aspects and methods that are necessary to develop your brand's image in this section.

Defining Your Brand Identity:

Vision, Mission and Values values and vision of your SMMA should be established in the first place. What goals do you want to achieve, and what are the principles that will guide the way you conduct yourself? The mission statement and the vision statement must be clearly stated.

Targeting Audience Determine which market segment you are targeting and find out about their requirements preference, habits, and challenges. By gaining this knowledge you are able to alter your content and messages so that you appeal to your targeted group of customers.

Unique Selling Proposition (USP) A USP (unique selling concept) Find the distinctive selling point for your SMMA. To differentiate your company be clear about what you want to convey and clearly state the unique value offering.

Creating a Compelling Brand Story:

Storytelling: Write an intriguing story about your SMMA. Retell the audience the story of the reasons you established the company and highlight your passion knowledge, expertise, and commitment to delivering results for your clients.

Brand Voice and Tone: Create the tone and persona of your business. What voice do you choose to use such as a warm, friendly one, a confident, or a creative one? One of the most crucial aspects to successful brand communications is consistency.

Designing Your Brand Identity:

Logo design: Develop an attractive and memorable logo that conveys all the essentials of your business. If you want to create the perfect logo for the brand's image, consider hiring a professional designer, or using websites for help.

Color Palette: Choose the color scheme that is appealing to your market segment and reflects what you want to convey with your company. Choose hues that fit for your particular industry and create the appropriate feelings.

Typeface: Select accessible fonts that will work to the various media, and convey the style of your business. When it comes to headings, subheadings or body content, consider using different fonts.

Visual Style Guide: Develop a visual style manual which outlines how your company's visual elements, like color schemes, logo positioning or typography guidelines, as well as images, must be applied consistently. This means that your branding will remain recognized and consistent across different media.

Consistent Branding Across Channels:

Website: Create your website with a professional look that captures all the essentials of your business. It should be easy for users to use, pleasing to the eye, and includes complete information on your product as well as your expertise.

Social Media Profiles: Optimize your social media profiles to ensure that they are a reflection of the character of your company. On platforms such as Facebook, Instagram, LinkedIn and Twitter Use unified graphics as well as messaging and voice.

Content Marketing Develop an effective content strategy that is reflective of the core values of your business and appeals to your intended audience. Make interesting and relevant media, like informationgraphics, podcasts, videos and blog entries.

Customer Experience: At each touchpoint, you should provide your customers an consistent, exceptional service. You must ensure that your clients' onboarding, customer support, and communications reflect your values and professionalism. your company.

It takes time and persistence to build a solid brand. You can create a trusted and easily identifiable SMMA brand that attracts clients and differentiates your brand from the crowd following these rules while staying loyal to the brand's image.

Creating Your LLC

Forming a legal entity to your business, for example the Limited Liability Company (LLC) is an option that's popular for establishing your own SMMA (Social Media Marketing Agency). This chapter guides you through each step to create your LLC.

Chapter 2: Opening Up Your Bank Account

It's essential to open an account for business banking when you've established that your SMMA (Social Media Marketing Agency) has been recognized as legally recognized as a distinct company. In this chapter, we will guide you through the steps to open a corporate bank account that will enhance the management of your finances and ensure that the personal and business accounts distinct.

Research and Choose the Right Bank:

Take a look at the Business Banking Options: Choose the financial institution or bank most suitable for your needs for an SMMA through a thorough study of these. Search for banks offering business-specific services and have reasonable costs, user-friendly internet banking along with other services to meet your specific needs.

Examine Account Types Select the bank for business account that's ideal to suit your SMMA. An account for business checks as well as a savings or checking account or a mixture of both are the most common options. Consider things such as minimal balance requirements as well as transaction fees in addition to interest rates and other features, such as mobile banking and merchant services.

Gather the Required Documentation:

"Employer Identification Number (EIN) This is the Internal Revenue Service (IRS) will give you the Employer Identification Number (EIN). An account for business banking should usually be established prior to you can request this particular identification number.

Business formation documents Prepare the documents required that prove the SMMA's existence as a legal business entity. These could be your permits and licences for business and Articles of Organization (for the LLC).

Personal identification: Get your personal identification papers like your driver's license or passport. You can also get a Social Security number for every participant in the SMMA.

Schedule an Appointment:

Call the Bank Get in touch with the bank you prefer and schedule a meeting with them to establish a business bank account. When you do this, will be able to ensure that an authorized staff member will be available to guide you through the process.

Visit the Bank and Complete the Application Process:

Attend appointment Then, visit the bank according to set, bring the required documents and identification.

Fill out the Application Forms Fill out the required applications forms that the bank has supplied. Name of your business, address, EIN and the ownership structure of the SMMA are among the data to be included on these forms.

Depositing Initial Funds: Deposit money to your company's new bank account. Based on the bank you use and accounts type, the needed amount could be different.

Set Up Online Banking and Additional Services:

"Online Banking": Make use of the internet-based banking options. This can be used to manage your business's finances, check the history of transactions as well as pay your bills and pay bills electronically.

Additional Services: Explore the additional offerings offered by banks such as business credit cards Merchant services to take payments and various other financial instruments to aid you with your SMMA.

Maintain Clear Financial Records:

Bookkeeping: Design an efficient system to maintain updated and exact financial record. This involves tracking the amount of money earned, expenditures, as well as regular bank reconciliation. Consider using an accounting program or partnering in conjunction with a professional bookkeeper.

Regular Review of Accounts For ensuring proper cash management, you must identify any fraud, and also be aware of any fees or costs, you should regularly monitor your bank account for business.

For a simpler managing your finances, and to ensure your business and personal finances remain distinct, it is recommended to create a separate business bank account to fund your SMMA. It is possible to establish a strong financial base for your business following these guidelines. If you need advice tailored to the specific needs of your business and the statutory regulations you should consider talking to an accountant or a financial consultant.

Niche Selection

The most important step to your success with an SMMA (Social Media Marketing Agency) is deciding on an area of interest. It is possible to tailor your services as well as your messaging and marketing actions to suit the unique requirements and needs of the niche you are in when you choose a certain sector or target market that you wish that you want to focus on. The guide will walk you by the steps of selecting the appropriate specific niche to an SMMA in this section.

Research and Identify Potential Niches:

Explore your interests and Skills: Start with a thought about your personal hobbies, interests and specializations. What industries or markets are you familiar with and are eager to get involved in? Finding the right market for your skills and preferences can improve your performance and improve your chances of achieving success.

Market Demand and Viability Examine market demand as well as the potential viability of your niche. Discover industries and markets which are growing, have an extensive presence on the internet, and show a need for the services of social media marketers. To identify opportunities analyze competitive research, market research as well as industry trends.

Evaluate Niche Characteristics:

Targeted Audience Think about the demographics and psychographics of the potential target market for each niche. Who would be your ideal customer precisely? In order to determine whether their requirements are in line with your offerings and capabilities take a look at their requirements concerns, preferences, and problems.

Competitive Analysis: Identify the amount of competition within each area by conducting a competition analysis. Examine the quality and quantity of SMMA businesses already on the market. Examine whether you are able to distinguish yourself by offering customers with a unique benefit who are in this particular segment.

Revenue and Profitability Consider the potential for profitability and potential revenue for every niche. Be aware of factors like the size of your market and your capacity to establish reasonable prices and also the likelihood of earning new business as well as forming solid relationships with your customers.

Narrow Down and Select Your Niche:

Take into consideration your expertise and passion Consider the areas which match your interest expertise, experience, and knowledge. Your enthusiasm and commitment to the work you do will stay at a high level if you choose the area of interest that really interests you.

Unique Value Proposition Consider how you can market your SMMA as an unique useful solution within your specific area. Consider the unique abilities, skills or strategies that you have to offer that will set yourself out from your competitors.

Long-term growth potential Choose areas that aren't overly saturated, and that have the potential for the long term expansion. In order to ensure that your selected area of interest is relevant and profitable be sure to consider the new trends and markets, and shifting markets' needs.

Refine Your Marketing Strategy:

Targeted messaging: the process of developing specific marketing communications and materials which are relevant to the requirements and challenges of your particular area is referred to as "targeted messaging." It shows that you're conscious of their issues and the ways you can assist by tailoring your message towards the audience you want to reach.

Marketing channels that are specific to niches Choose which niche-specific marketing channels are able to help you reach your intended audience. It could be a combination of specific sites, social media platforms specifically targeted to an industry or events for networking. Make sure you are focusing your marketing efforts on those platforms that connect and get your desired audience engaged most effectively.

Partnerships and Networking Participate in gatherings for networking and build alliances with people in your chosen niche. Establish connections with thought leaders and influential individuals in the business, and prospective clients in order to establish your credibility and establish your presence on the market.

Careful research and thought is necessary when choosing a topic that you can use as your SMMA. Your agency can be positioned as a specialist service company and attract clients who appreciate your knowledge by picking an area that's the same direction as your passions knowledge, experience, and potential. In order to ensure that you continue the expansion and the success of your SMMA regularly review and adjust your strategy for niche in line with market trends.

Creating Your Offer

In order for the success of your SMMA (Social Media Marketing Agency) to attract and retain customers, it is essential to craft an appealing and compelling offer. In this article we'll look at the fundamental steps to create an offer that highlights the unique value of your business and is tailored to the needs of your market.

Understand Client Needs and Pain Points:

"Market Research": Perform thorough market research to discover the exact requirements, obstacles and apprehensions of your intended audience in the framework of your selected field. This allows you to focus on the issues they face and provide useful solutions to them in your offering.

Surveys and interviews with clients Interview prospective customers during interviews or in surveys for a clear insight into their wants such as preferences, expectations, and needs. This allows you to Improve the way you tailor your service according to the needs of your customers.

Define Your Service Offerings:

*Core Services Select the most fundamental of services to constitute the foundation of your SMMA. It could include community management analysis as well as influencer marketing. It could also include managing social media as well as content creation and campaign management, or any mixture of these.

Options for Customization Consider offering diverse packages and options to customize based on the various requirements and financial budgets of your customers. It allows you to provide a customized approach, and appeal to different client groups.

Other Value-Added Services Choose additional services or distinct services that could make your business stand out from competitors. These could be branding services such as training courses and market research. It could also include competitor analysis and strategic consultation.

Pricing and Packaging:

Pricing Strategy: Create an effective pricing plan that is and is competitive as well as in keeping with your value proposition. Take into consideration your expertise area as well as industry standards and the amount of job, and your desired outcome.

"Package Options: Design diverse packages to fit the requirements and budgets of different customers. Every package must specify what services are offered as well as the dates for completion of them, and the price, as well as any other terms and terms.

Tiered pricing: You might consider choosing tiered pricing plans with different degrees of service and prices. It allows customers to choose the plan that is most suitable for the needs of their business while encouraging the possibility of upgrades and even upsells.

Communicate Your Unique Value Proposition:

Clear Benefits: In a clear manner, define the benefits and value customers will gain when they select your SMMA. Make sure to emphasize how your products can solve their issues and improve their online presence and increase awareness of their brand as well as encourage sales. You can also achieve other goals.

Case studies and testimonials to demonstrate the worth of your products, you should highlight your previous successes and the endorsements of clients. Provide concrete examples of results and achievements to build trust and credibility.

"Differentiation: Be clear about the things that distinguish your business from your competitors. Unique selling points like your expert understanding of the industry and innovative approaches, as well as exceptional customer service must be highlighted.

Develop Compelling Sales Materials:

Sales Presentations: Design attractive and informative sales presentation that highlights important characteristics, benefits and successes of your SMMA. These presentations should be unique to certain industries or clienteles.

Proposals and contracts Make professional contracts and proposals that outline the terms, conditions, deliverables as well as deadlines and the cost of the services you offer. In order to avoid misunderstandings and disputes be sure to provide transparency and clarity.

Marketing Collateral: Develop marketing collateral that communicate clearly your expertise and value the service you offer. Examples include catalogs, cases as well as one-pagers. To draw attention and entice the attention of potential customers, you should use convincing words and pictures.

Understanding the target market the needs of your target audience, as well as the value that you could offer for them to make an attractive offering. Create an offering that is unique on the market, and draw people to your SMMA through matching your service prices, marketing, and communications strategies to the needs of your customers. To make sure that your proposition remains effective and relevant regularly review it and adjust it based on the feedback of customers and trends in the market.

Chapter 3: Setting Up Your Tech Stack

To simplify your operation and increase the effectiveness in Your SMMA (Social Media Marketing Agency) it is essential to set your organization with a reliable and productive technology stack. In this section we'll look at the most important components of a technology stack and help you choose the right tools available to your company in use.

Assess Your Agency's Needs:

Examine Workflow and Processes: Review your company's processes and workflow for areas in which technology could improve efficiency and speed up processes. Include activities like the development of content and social media management, projects administration and analytics, communication and report-writing.

Find the Pain Points That is, identify the issues and problems you face in the daily tasks you carry out. It could relate to issues that involve teamwork, content management or data analysis, client communications, or any other circumstance where technology could aid in solving the problem.

Selecting Tools for Your Tech Stack:

Social Media Management Choose a reliable social media management software which allows you to interact with your target audience, develop and post content on various social media platforms, as well as monitor results measures. Hootsuite, Buffer, and Sprout Social are a few examples.

Design and Content Creation Utilize design and content creation tools, like applications for graphic design, such as Canva as well as Adobe Creative Cloud, to create visually pleasing and captivating video content. When creating videos you should think about using software that include Adobe Premiere Pro or Final Cut Pro.

Project Management: In order to manage and manage the due dates, tasks and timelines of projects to your team, pick an application for managing projects. The most popular choices are Monday.com, Asana, and Trello.

Collaboration and Communication Select a platform that allows effective files sharing, instant communication and collaboration between team members. Slack, Microsoft Teams, and Google Workspace are a few instances.

Analytics and Reporting Make use of tools such as Google Analytics, Sprout Social and SEMrush to monitor and analyze the analytics of social media and websites. They provide insightful information about audience reach, conversions as well as other important indicators.

Customer Relationship Management (CRM) It is worth making use of a client relation management (CRM) tool to monitor the customer relationship, monitor leads and track the pipeline for sales. CRMs like Salesforce, HubSpot, or Zoho CRM are some examples of typical CRM systems.

Integration and Automation:

Seamless Integration seamless flow of data and platforms-to-platform collaboration is possible through the use of tools which can be integrated easily with one another. With the elimination of the manual entry of data This integration increases productivity.

Automation: Use your automation tools within your stack of tech to reduce the time spent on repetitive jobs. For instance, this could mean creating reports, automating email campaigns or scheduling posts for social media.

Implementation and Training:

Implementation Plan: Design an implementation plan for your stack of technology that takes into consideration factors like training for users as well as data migration and the gradual introduction of technology to minimize disruption.

User Training and Support Help and Training for Users Team members must be given thorough instructions regarding how to use the software in your stack. Utilize the user guides for training, materials for instructors, or online tutorials from the company.

Evaluate and Evolve:

Regular evaluation: Always examine the efficiency of your technology stack and the tools you use. Collect the opinions of the team members on the areas that need improvement and consider adding new features or devices to meet the needs of your business.

Keep up-to-date: Stay abreast of the most recent advancements in business and technology developments. Explore new integrations, features and software that could enhance the efficiency of your agency and keep it in the game.

Your efficiency and productivity of your organization is significantly enhanced when installing a complete technological stack. It is possible to streamline your processes and offer your customers superior service by deciding and applying the right tools, effortlessly linking platforms, and delivering all the training you need. As you expand your business and technology improves, you should periodically evaluate and update your technology system to ensure that your company is at the cutting edge of your industry.

8. 8. Scrape Your ListA crucial step in the achievement of your SMMA (Social Media Marketing Agency) is the creation of an outstanding contact lists. Scraping your list, which entails collecting relevant contact details through various sources online, will be discussed in this section. This list is the foundation of your outreach and marketing projects.

Define Your Target Audience:

Based on your industry and the products you offer to your customers, you must clearly define your ideal customers. Determine the characteristics, demographics as well as the specific requirements which define your ideal customers.

Select Suitable Sources for Data:

Social Media platforms: Investigate the social networks in which your public is likely to be like LinkedIn, Facebook, Instagram, Twitter, or industry-specific platforms.

Look for business directories specifically tailored to your field or directories of business that include companies or experts in your targeted market.

Forums and Online Communities You can join online communities, forums, or communities that relate to the niche you are in. They often provide helpful contacts for those curious about your field.

Web Scraping Tools: Think about utilizing web scraping software or other tools for extracting the data from web pages as well as other online platforms. They can speed up the process and can automate it.

Identify and Extract Contact Information:

Titles and names Note the names and titles of people who satisfy the needs of your public. This information will allow you to customize your outreach activities.

"Company Information: Collect data about businesses or organizations that your targeted market falls under. Names, addresses and web addresses of companies are listed.

Email Addresses: Find email addresses from a number of sites, including directories of businesses as well as social media profiles and Contact pages. For the purpose of reaching out to communicate with one another the email address is essential.

"Social Media" Profiles Get the profile or link to the target markets' social media accounts. They can be interacting with you directly through these social media platforms due to this data.

Check for compliance Data Privacy Regulations:

Find out about the rules and regulations that govern data privacy within the region you work in in. Be sure the data scraping processes you use comply with these guidelines.

Follow the guidelines: Read the platform's guidelines and terms of service guidelines while scraping data off them. Pay attention to any limitations or restrictions they may have imposed on you by their platforms.

Request Permission to Direct Contact: Once you've collected contact details, you must respect the privacy laws and seek consent prior to contacting someone directly, or including them on your list of email addresses.

Chapter 4: Outreach

1: Setting up Outreach - Email

One of the most effective ways to get in touch with prospective clients and to generate prospects for the SMMA (Social Media Marketing Agency) is through implementing an effective email outreach plan. In this article we'll review the fundamental methods for designing email outreach strategies that draw the interest of recipients and result in successful results.

Define Your Outreach Goals:

Set your goals for email outreach with specificity. Do you want to draw new customers, develop relations, advertise your offerings, or build leads? Your approach and message is based on having a the same goal.

Build a Targeted Email List:

Make use of the contacts list you've collected through scraping or by other methods. Check to see if the individuals you've selected meet the requirements of your intended audience and are interested for your product or industry.

Segment Your List Divide your list into sections by relevant elements such as work title, industry or even location. This lets you create personalised messages and content that is tailored to your needs.

Choose an Email Service Provider (ESP):

Select an email provider that has an excellent reputation that offers services like personalization, tracking as well as automated email to increase the quality of your emails. Mailchimp Constant Contact as well as Sendinblue are some of the most famous ESPs.

To ensure that your outreach emails the most efficient be familiar with the capabilities and features of the ESP you prefer. ESP.

Craft Compelling Email Copy:

Personalization: By calling the recipients with their name and altering the contents to meet all concerns or requirements that they might have You can customize your email messages. Unpersonalized and generic tend to not get a good response.

Attention-grabbing subject lines Create concise, eye-catching as well as specific to the recipient. The likelihood of opening emails is higher when your subject line is interesting.

Engaging email Body An engaging email body Design an email body that concise and convincing clear in communicating your proposition of value, eases the reader's fears and entices the recipient to take action. Concentrate on the benefits instead of the features, and employ a conversational approach.

Call-to Action (CTA) include the call-to action (CTA) that is easily recognizable and well-known and directs users to perform the desired action like making a phone call or downloading an item, or visiting your site. Create a way to make the CTA visible.

Automation and Follow-Up:

Email sequences Make use of automated email to create drip-campaigns or email sequences which send recipients focused emails for a certain duration. This allows you to keep in touch with leads and keep them engaged.

Follow-up Emails: Send emails to those who haven't responded to your initial call. The emails could address issues and offer rewards to encourage responses, or provide additional details.

Monitor, Analyze, and Optimise:

Keep track of Email Metrics: Use the analytics of your email provider to monitor the most important metrics in email, such as the number of open, click through rate as well as conversion rates. These statistics provide insight into the success of your marketing campaigns.

A/B testing For the best results from your outreach, try different subject lines for emails in the form of content iterations or CTAs. For a comparison of the effectiveness of the various elements and enhance your approach, perform A/B tests.

Continuous Improvement: Examine your results from outreach emails regularly. Find areas of enhancement, and learn from your failures and successes and modify your strategies according to customer feedback and the level of engagement.

Be sure to adhere to the most effective practices when it comes to email marketing. This includes obtaining permission, and providing an easy unsubscribe option. In order to maintain a good image and ensure compliance to relevant regulations, you must respect the privacy of recipients and their preferences. Engage with prospective customers, build relationships as well as increase the number of conversions to your SMMA through a smart approach to email outreach.

Setting Up Outreach - DMs

For various the social networks, direct messages (DM) is an effective method of connecting with prospective clients and for establishing meaningful connections. In this article we'll review the most important methods for creating direct mail campaigns that are successful in attracting recipients and result in leads to you to use for your SMMA (Social Media Marketing Agency).

Select Suitable Social Media Platforms:

Select the platforms on social media that your market segment is engaged. Consider active platforms on which the potential customers are for example, LinkedIn, Instagram, Facebook, Twitter, or industry-specific platforms.

Define Your DM Outreach Goals:

Determine the purpose for your DM outreach efforts in depth. Are you looking to introduce yourself, build relations, schedule calls to sell or arrange meetings? The way you communicate and the strategy for it is guided by a an objective.

Research and Identify Targeted Individuals:

To identify those who fit the criteria of your intended market, conduct thorough study. For prospective customers or key decision makers within organizations, look up relevant hashtags, industries groups or community.

Be attentive to those who are active in your website, show enthusiasm for your industry or have a demand to purchase your product or service. Your DM outreach is likely to be appreciated by those who are.

Personalise Your DMs:

Personalize the contents of your DMs for the individual recipients. Start by giving the recipient's names. Then, include details that prove you've studied the subject and understand the needs of each recipient.

Be wary of sending unpersonal or generic messages that seem as if they were sent by an automated system. In order to stand out and create a trust with your individual who received the message, personalization is crucial.

Craft Compelling DM Content:

Engaging Opening: Start your message directly with captivating and warm introduction. It should be clear you're able to help people and be conscious of their issues or goals.

Value Proposition The client will gain from your assistance by being transparent in the way you communicate the SMMA's distinctive value proposition. In order to establish trust and credibility emphasize tangible results or stories of success.

Call-to Action (CTA) include a persuasive call to action (CTA) which encourages your recipient to complete the desired action. It could involve calling or visiting your site or engaging in a lengthy discussion.

Follow-Up and Nurture Relationships:

Make a plan for follow-up to keep in touch with those who initially showed desire to or commitment. This could include sending further DMs that contain helpful info such as links or other offers which are specific to the individual who received it.

Be patient and persistent and do not be excessively pushy or aggressive. Take into consideration the time of the receiver and needs while building a rapport that is beneficial for both sides.

Monitor, Analyze, and Optimise:

Monitor the DM outreach efforts' response and response rates is crucial. In order to gauge the effectiveness of your outreach efforts make sure you keep track of the metrics such as response rate or conversation frequency, as well as conversion rates.

Determine which messages resonate best with the people you want to reach by examining your content, style, and frequency of your targeted messages.Try using different techniques for messaging before adjusting your approach as you need to in response to the feedback you receive and your performance.

Maintain Professionalism and Etiquette:

The way you handle DMs must always remain respectful and professional. Do not engage in any manner that might be perceived as intrusive or rude, for example the use of spam, excessive follow-ups etc.

Respond to any questions or concerns from the recipients as quickly as you can. Discuss important issues and contribute value to conversations that you engage in.

It is possible to connect with prospective customers, establish relationships as well as increase the conversion rate of your SMMA by using an expertly designed DM outreach plan. Remember to protect the privacy of your recipients and their preferences, and then adapt your strategy according to their feedback and engagement.

Setting Up Your Inbound Ads

An effective SMMA (Social Media Marketing Agency) method to attract potential clients and build leads is called inbound marketing. In this article we'll examine the fundamental steps to set an inbound marketing campaign that will effectively attract the target audience and steer your customers towards your offerings.

Define Your Inbound Advertising Goals:

Be clear about the purpose of your campaigns for inbound marketing. Are you trying to build leads, establish your brand image, market an item, or boost traffic to your website? Your approach and message is based on having the goal in mind.

Identify Your Target Audience:

Determine the exact qualities, attributes and the interests of the people you want to reach. For ads to be engaging and resonate with your target audience it is first necessary to understand their characteristics, traits, and interests.

Gain an comprehension of your audience through conducting market research, studying customer information, and making use of audience research accessible on online websites for ad campaigns.

Choose the Right Advertising Platforms:

To effectively get your message to the right public, select the channels that are most suitable for the needs of your audience. Google Ads, Facebook Ads, Instagram Ads, LinkedIn Ads along with YouTube Ads, are just a handful of popular channels for advertising.

When choosing the platform which are the best fit for your SMMA consider the advantages and benefits of each, like advertising formats, targeting options and the reach of your audience.

Develop Engaging Ad Creative:

Effective Copywriting: Create appealing and concise advertisement copy that captivates attention and communicates your unique worth proposition and inspires to take action. Use appealing headlines, succinct messages, and persuasive call to take action.

"Eye-Catching" Visuals Make visually appealing films or images which appeal to your intended audience and align with the brand's image. Use appealing design elements, appropriate images, and emotional imagery.

Try a variety of variations Test several headlines, photos and calls to actions within your ads. Improve your advertisement creativity by finding out which parts work best by testing A/B.

Set Up Targeting and Budgeting:

Define Targeting Criteria Make use of the targeting options available by the platforms that advertise for targeting certain demographics, interest behavior, behaviors or geographical areas of your target audience. In order to reach the best target audience to your SMMA refine your target audience.

Set a budget for advertising: Create an appropriate advertising budget that's aligned with your business goals and resources available. Make wise use of your budget by dividing it up into different campaigns, and watching the outcomes.

Monitor and Optimise Ad Performance:

Track important metrics Pay attention to the most important indicators like impressions clicks, conversions and click-through rates and costs per purchase to assess the performance of your online advertisements. These metrics will provide insight on the effectiveness of your ads. are.

Analyze and refine: Analyze and refine performance data over time for areas that might need improvement. Advertising can be more efficient through changing the options for targeting as well as the ad's copy. spend your budget on the results you observe.

Conversion Tracking Use the tools for tracking conversions to monitor the extent to which your advertisements result in desired actions for example, form submissions calls, or purchase. This helps you understand the extent of the ROI for your campaign.

Explore Ad Formats, and strategies

To broaden your online marketing, you can experiment with different ad formats and methods. These could be dynamic ads targeted to specific segments of the audience videos and carousel advertisements advertising lead generation, or Remarketing campaigns.

To make the most of innovative features and possibilities to improve the effectiveness of your online ad campaigns, keep up-to-date with the latest trends in the industry and updates to platforms.

It is possible to effectively connect with your intended audience, create good leads, and boost the profile of your SMMA with well-planned ads that target inbound traffic. For maximum impact from your advertising campaigns inbound constantly evaluate and enhance your advertising campaigns on the basis of the insights of your audience and data on performance.

Setting Up Your Content Flywheel

The content flywheel is an powerful strategy for producing relevant and engaging material to attract to, engage and maintain the attention of your intended viewers. This chapter will discuss the most important steps to set up the most effective content flywheel in you SMMA (Social Media Marketing Agency) in this section.

Define Your Content Goals:

Clearly state the objectives of the content flywheel. Are you looking to attract the audience, advertise your offerings, demonstrate an image of thought leadership or even inform your audience? Your strategy for creating content should be based on specific objectives.

Identify Your Target Audience:

Find out the specific qualities, attributes as well as the interests of the target group of readers. To ensure that your content resonates with your viewers and appeal to their concerns or interests It is crucial to know who they are.

To find out more about your target audience's tastes and requirements Conduct research on the market, study information about customers and then interact with them via survey or through social media listening.

Develop a Content Strategy:

Content Topics: Select relevant topics for content that are pertinent with your SMMA and appeal to the intended viewers. For help in creating your content, consider the latest trends in market, commonly asked questions, daily challenges, or new areas.

Formats for Content: Formats for Content Select the types of content most suitable for your readers' requirements and goals. These could be audio posts on social media, podcasts video, infographics or blog posts, as well as infographics. Make sure to create a variety of formats for content to meet different preferences.

Content Calendar Make an agenda for your content calendar and organize the production and dissemination of content. Set due dates, delegate the roles and ensure the constant flow of informational material.

Create High-Quality Content:

Relevant and Valuable Concentrate your efforts in creating content that is beneficial to the people who read it. Give your viewers useful details that can help users solve issues or meet their goals, for example professional advice, updates to industry or other educational materials.

Effective Headlines: Write appealing headlines that will encourage viewers to click on and engage with your website content. In order to entice them you can use convincing phrases, provocative topics or intriguing responses.

Visual Attraction: Visual Attraction Include eye-catching elements within your content including high-resolution photographs video, graphics, or photos. Visuals can increase the engagement of your audience and boost the sharing potential of your information.

SEO Optimization: by using relevant keyword phrases, metatags as well as headings that convey emotion and evocative, you can enhance your content to be friendly to search engines. This will increase your visibility and the ability to find your site's contents in result pages of search engines.

Distribute and Promote Your Content:

Channels for Social Media: Make sure to share your posts on appropriate social media platforms that your audience there. To reach more people you should use sites like LinkedIn, Facebook, Instagram, Twitter, or YouTube.

Marketing via email: Utilize your list of email addresses to connect with those who have expressed an desire to learn more about your SMMA and then distribute your content to those who have expressed interest. Make interesting newsletters for email or customized content recommendations to increase your readership.

Influencer Collaboration: In order to collaborate on or publish your own content, collaborate with influential people or industry experts. In this way it allows you to be more visible to a larger audience and build credibility.

Content syndication: You should think about publishing your content on reliable industry blogs, websites or content aggregaters. This allows you to connect with a bigger public and also draw backlinks to increase the ranking of your site.

Engage Your Audience

Encourage Interaction: Inspire audience interaction by inviting users to share, follow or leave a make comments about your blog posts. Create a sense of connection to your content through replying to comments or questions.

Chapter 5: Sales Calls

Setting Up Your Intro Call Script

The first phone call is a crucial step in the SMMA's (Social Media Marketing Agency) selling process. This is a chance for you to communicate with prospective customers, find out about their preferences and explain the ways your products can assist to achieve their goals. In this chapter, we will look at the most important aspects to be considered in the creation of your introduction phone script in this section.

Introduction and Warm Greeting:

Begin the call by greeting the caller with a warm and friendly greeting. Set a professional and friendly tone, immediately present yourself and the role you play as a representative of the agency.

Thank the prospective customer to thank them for their time, and also express gratitude for the chance to discuss how your company could assist you.

Establish Rapport and Build Trust:

Show genuine curiosity about the prospective's objectives and their company. Engage them in open-ended discussions to push people to talk about their issues or goals, as well as marketing-related problems.

Allow your prospect to express fully their desires in a manner that you pay attention and actively listen. This suggests that you are respectful of their perspective and are dedicated to understanding their specific situation.

Highlight Your Agency's Value Proposition:

Explain the SMMA's unique benefit in simple language. In your pitch, highlight the ways your business stands out against the rest and also what you can do to assist your prospect solve their specific needs or desires.

Include the case studies, successes stories or testimonials from clients to show the success that you've achieved for previous clients. This improves the credibility of your company and increases confidence in your capabilities.

Tailor Your Solution to Their Needs:

Create a plan which is adapted to meet the specific needs of your prospect and requirements using the data you learned from the discussion. Make sure you highlight the specific program or strategies that meet their requirements.

Describe how your business could provide a bespoke approach that solves their issues and helps them achieve what they need. It is important to emphasize your advantages from working with your agency.

Address Potential Concerns or Objections:

Be aware of and respond to any concerns or doubts that the prospective client might have. In order to dispel doubts and show your knowledge Prepare succinct and persuasive answers.

Answer questions about cost or deadlines for delivery or any other concerns that may influence the decision of the prospective client.

Discuss Next Steps:

The next step of the sales procedure with specificity. It could include setting up the call to follow up and providing more information or details, or even presenting an offer or contract.

Identify the timeframes and steps that each party is expected to be able to take. Be sure that the prospective client is informed of the process and feels at ease with the process.

Be sure to reiterate your excitement to work with the prospective partner as you thank the potential partner for your time. In order to ensure they understand what was discussed during the meeting, write down your main details.

A clearly defined message should be utilized to end the phone call. This could include making arrangements for a follow-up phone call or handing over certain documents or information. Be sure that the prospective customer is aware of how to reach you should they have additional queries or would like to proceed in the next step.

Continuous Improvement:

The script for your intro calls must be reviewed regularly and adapted based on client feedback, the results of sales and the areas to be developed. In order to better satisfy the requirements and needs of your customers change the call script.

To find effective strategies to improve the effectiveness of your program, ask your sales personnel to discuss their experience as well as their insights on the first call.

An organized and engaging discussion with customers who are interested in your services can be made by preparing the perfect intro-call script. Write a script that outlines your unique selling points of your business, addresses customer concerns and provides how to proceed during the sales process. In order to improve your sales strategies and increase your conversion rate continue to improve your writing.

Setup The demo presentation provides an excellent opportunity to demonstrate potential customers the advantages and expertise from your SMMA (Social Media Marketing Agency). This allows you to provide an explanation in pictures of your products and services, outline your strategies, and reply to any concerns or questions you might get. The following chapter will discuss the essential elements to consider in arranging your demo phone presentation in this section.

Introduction and Agenda:

Introduce yourself and explain your job within the agency before commencing the talk. Begin with a tone that's positive and exciting.

Outline the demo's program in great detail. This provides the structure of the presentation and helps establish expectations.

Understand the Prospect's Goals:

Recall the main objectives and concerns raised in the opening meeting. Make sure you pay attentively to the issues and have a clear understanding of the specific needs of each person.

Please describe in detail the ways your organization can help the team in reaching their goals and overcome their obstacles.

Overview of Your Agency:

Write a brief overview of your business by highlighting your expertise of experience, expertise, and achievements. Concentrate on your company's distinctive selling point and what they do to differentiate it from other companies.

Display any awards and certifications or associations specific to your industry which prove your company's experience and credibility.

Demonstrate Your Services:

Give an overview of your services. Define each service's connection to the goals of your customers and the ways they could make use of it.

Utilize successful stories, case studies or even before-and-after cases to show how your products and services are affecting client-specific campaigns. It is possible to make your presentation better if you include pictures or graphs.

Walkthrough of Your Strategies:

Describe the strategies and methods your firm employs to achieve the goals of your clients. Provide details on your research methods to analyze your customer's needs to create content and optimize your marketing campaign.

Give an example of the your most successful campaigns as well as the outcomes that they generated. It shows how adept your company is at generating real positive results.

Address Questions and Concerns:

Through the talk, you should encourage your audience to inquire. Respond quickly and in a concise manner as well as promptly respond to any concerns they have.

Be ready to respond frequently to defenses or issues that customers who are interested in your services might be facing. Offer arguments or answers in order to dispel any suspicion that they might have.

Customization and Personalization:

Display how your organization is able to adjust its strategies and marketing in order to satisfy the specific needs of each customer. Demonstrate the flexibility to modify your strategies to meet the needs specific to the potential client.

Discuss how you interact with clients in order to ensure their branding voice, message as well as campaign objectives are successfully incorporated.

Call-to-Action and Next Steps:

The next stages should be described in detail. This could include presenting an extensive proposition, contract or pricing details.

If a prospect seems ready to take action, help them to follow through by scheduling a phone call to follow-up, or by having them to sign the agreement.

Conclusion and Thank You:

Recall the major themes that were discussed in the talk. Highlight the value and benefits the agency could provide.

Please thank the prospective client for their time and opportunity to discuss your offerings. Let them know you are excited about your potential partnership.

Continuous Improvement:

Re-evaluate and refine the demo presentation you have created regularly according to customer feedback as well as the results of your sales as well as areas of improvement. The content of the presentation and its flow must be adjusted so that it can better suit the requirements and needs of the customers you are trying to attract.

To discover effective methods and increase your overall performance in your demonstration, get your sales staff to share their experience and knowledge during demonstration calls.

Effectively highlight the strengths of your company and draw in potential clients with an organized and engaging demonstration call. Make sure that the presentation is tailored to meet the needs and goals of the prospective client, as well as highlighting the advantages of your services.

Chapter 6: Learning The Sales Process

To allow you and your SMMA (Social Media Marketing Agency) to achieve success it is essential to understand and be able to master the selling process. It involves carefully guiding potential customers through all stages of the selling process beginning with making the initial call until closing the sale. This chapter will examine the most important aspects in this section as we learn about the sales procedure for your company.

Prospecting and Lead Generation:

Identify and reach potential customers that could benefit by your company's offerings. This is possible with lead generation strategies via networking, internet, or market analysis.

Make a database of leads, which includes important contact details and information on the challenges and needs faced by their business.

Qualifying Leads:

Leads must be assessed and evaluated to determine whether they are in line with your company's customers and really need the services of your agency. It involves evaluating aspects such as their budget plan goals, timetable and their alignment with the expertise of your agency.

Prioritize leads according to the potential value they could bring by applying lead scoring methods or by asking questions that are relevant to the first conversations.

Needs Assessment:

The leads should be evaluated and evaluated to determine whether they match with your organization's customers and really need the services of your agency. This involves looking at elements such as the budget goals, timetable as well as their compatibility with your expertise.

The priority of leads is based on their value potential employing lead scoring or asking relevant questions in the first conversations.

Presenting Solutions:

Adjust recommendations and strategies according to the requirements of the potential customer. Discuss how the services of your company will help them solve the issues they face and achieve their goals.

The advantages as well as the ROI (Return on investment) when cooperating with your agency must be made clear in persuasive presentation, proposals or in demonstrations.

Handling Objections:

Recognize potential issues or objections from potential clients and address them. This requires the ability to listen with a sense of empathy, and the ability to present powerful arguments.

Create rebuttals and case studies to address objections that are common and show your organization as the most effective solution to their issues.

Closing the Deal:

Request the prospective client to sign a contract with the services provided by your agency in the future. It could involve discussions about pricing options, negotiation of the terms of service, and addressing any questions that arise in the last minutes.

To convince the potential client to take a final decision, convey the impression of urgency, and emphasize the unique importance of your company.

Follow-Up and Relationship Building:

Stay in contact regularly with customers that are interested in your products but don't have a decision yet. In order to keep the connection keep in touch with them by providing more information, case studies or suggestions.

Continue to help existing clients, produce outcomes, and look out for potential referrals or opportunities for upselling, and build your relationship to them with time.

Continuous Improvement:

Review and evaluate the sales process regularly to identify areas where it can be made better. Keep track of conversion rates, keep an in mind key performance indicators, and ask your sales team's opinions.

Provide your sales staff with regularly scheduled opportunities to grow professionally as well as training and development to enhance their capabilities and understand effective sales techniques.

Increase the conversion rate improve sales efficiency and convince potential clients of the benefits of your SMMA products by gaining knowledge how to implement the right sales procedures. For the best results, tailor your sales processes to suit the needs specific to the market you want to target.

Practice

In order to master the sales procedure to run you SMMA (Social Media Marketing Agency) it is important to practice. It helps you refine your skills, increase confidence in yourself, and increase your ability to effectively communicate with possible clients. This chapter will explore how important it is to practice, and provide tips regarding how to practice successfully.

Role-Playing:

Play various sales scenarios alongside your sales team, or your mentors. You can play the roles of the salesperson and prospective customer in alternating fashion.

Practice handling critics, making presentations and addressing frequent questions. This will put you comfortable and prepared to engage in real-life interactions with potential clients.

Mock Sales Calls:

Practice selling calls with colleagues or team members that will act as prospective clients. They should be recorded and analyzed for areas that require improvement.

Be aware of your speech quality, tone as well as your active listening capabilities as well as your capacity to effectively communicate your importance to the service offered by your organization.

Feedback and Evaluation:

Ask colleagues, mentors or salespeople who are knowledgeable for opinions. They are able to provide insightful suggestions and constructive critique to identify your strengths as well as areas of improvement.

Check out recordings of sales calls or presentation to evaluate your effectiveness. Review your communication clarity as well as your ability to manage the objections.

Continuous Learning:

Stay informed about new trends in sales, business strategies and the best practices. For a better understanding and skills, take part in seminars, webinars or sales-related training programs.

Learn persuasive communication techniques strategy, negotiation techniques, and selling techniques through articles, books, as well as blogs. Utilize the knowledge you've gained in the sessions you practice.

Role-Modeling:

Learn the strategies that successful salespeople use or the methods used by coaches. Study their techniques, style of speaking and building rapport techniques with potential clients.

Copy their strategies that have worked and implement them in your own plan of action. Implement their tactics into your sales talks through practice.

Refine Your Pitch:

Continue to improve the message and sales pitch that you utilize. Focus on explaining your company's unique benefits and the value of their services with clarity.

Practice presenting your pitch clearly and convincing manner. Remove jargon and alter the message to ensure it appeals to your target audience.

Time Management:

Utilize time management methods to deal with customers. Find a way to the right balance between giving insightful feedback as well as advancing the dialogue.

Be careful not to talk about too much or provide prospects with excessive information. Engage them effectively while paying consideration to their preferences and paying attention to their needs and respecting their time.

Confidence Building:

Increase your confidence by working out. You'll feel more confident and confident during interactions with salespeople the more you work on and perfect the sales strategies you employ.

Have confidence in the quality of your company and the products you offer. Be professional and maintain an optimistic attitude during your sales procedure.

Remember that practice is a continual procedure. Participate in regular practice sessions, ask for feedback and constantly improve the sales techniques you employ. You'll improve your capacity to control your sales processes and improve the likelihood of turning prospective customers to clients to your SMMA through consistent commitment and effort.

Service Delivery

Setting Up Client Ads on TikTok

TikTok is a popular social media platform that is growing rapidly and holds huge potential as advertisements for corporations. How to set the client advertisements on TikTok to promote the purposes of your SMMA (Social Media Marketing Agency) will be discussed in this section. Utilizing the advertising capabilities of TikTok will enable you to reach out to an enormous audience, as well as increase engagement with your clients as well as conversions.

Understand TikTok Advertising:

Find out about the different TikTok advertising possibilities available. These include branding takeovers, brand effects as well as in-feed ads as well as other.

Learn about options for targeting as well as bidding strategies and ad formats that can help you create effective advertising campaigns that will benefit your customers.

Define Advertising Goals:

Define your client's TikTok marketing goals by working closely with the client. It is vital to know their goals in creating effective ads that are successful in creating leads, or increasing web traffic, app downloads or brand recognition.

Match your advertising goals with the market you are targeting for your client and expected results.

Set Up a TikTok Ads Account:

When you go to the TikTok Ads Manager's site to sign up to get an TikTok ads account. In order to register your company and access TikTok Ads, make sure you submit the necessary details.

To have a seamless advertising experience, be sure to follow TikTok's policies on advertising and rules.

Create a Campaign:

Within the TikTok Ads Manager, you can begin with a brand new campaign. Select an objective for example, reaching, traffic, or conversions that are compatible with your client's marketing goals.

Based on factors like location, age and gender, as well as interests and habits, you can define your people you want to reach.

TikTok has a wide range of ways to target users with users who are relevant.

Design Compelling Ad Creative:

Design captivating and attractive ad ideas to capture TikTok viewers to pay focus. For your ads to stick out, make use of TikTok's distinct artistic features such as effects, music as well as filters.

Ad-creative must be consistent to the branding of your client message, as well as the target preference of the audience.

Optimise Ad Placements:

Depending on the goal and budget of your client, choose the most effective ad spots. TikTok offers options such as challenge hashtags with sponsored hashtags advertising in feeds and branding effects.

To determine the most effective advertising placements to meet the goals of your client's campaign Try a range of possibilities.

Set Budget and Bidding Strategy:

Make sure you have enough money set aside to fund the TikTok advertisement campaign to your customer. When deciding on the budget, you should take into account factors like time frame, its reach and the expected outcome.

Based on the needs of your clients' goals and the budget available choose the most effective bidding method, for example cost per click (CPM) as well as cost per click (CPC).

Monitor and Optimise:

Be vigilant at the performance of your clients' TikTok marketing campaigns. Examine important metrics such as impressions or clicks, engagement level as well as converts.

To improve the effectiveness of your campaign, identify improvements and make the data-driven changes. Changes in targeting, strategy, or creative could be a part of this.

Report and Client Communication:

Provide clients with detailed reports on performance that outline crucial metrics and information. Send the TikTok advertising campaign's results, and suggest ideas for the future campaign.

All through the course of your campaign, remain constantly in communication with your customers and answer any questions or concerns that they might need to address.

The platform can help you reach a wider public and deliver more visible positive results for your business when you set up ads for clients on TikTok. In order to create compelling ads which connect to users on the platform, keep current on the latest TikTok advertising capabilities and the best practices. To maximize the ROI it is essential to continuously monitor your progress, adjust, and report about the success of their TikTok marketing campaigns.

Setting Up Client Ads on Facebook

A single of the best and most successful marketing platforms that can be used by companies that are of any size is still be Facebook. In this chapter, we will provide more details on how you can set up clients' Facebook ads to promote the purposes of your SMMA (Social Media Marketing Agency) in this section. Effectively get your message to the right audience for your client as well as encourage conversions and engagement through Facebook's extensive targeting options and advertising capabilities.

Understand Facebook Advertising:

Discover the many Facebook advertising options accessible. This includes video ads chat ads, carousel advertisements, feed ads as well as more.

For effective advertising campaigns for clients, know about the different formats for ads including targeting choices, as well as bidding strategies.

Define Advertising Goals:

Work with your client in defining the Facebook goals for advertising. It is vital to know their objectives in creating successful ads that are effective in boosting sales, creating leads or building brand awareness.

Match your advertising goals with the market you are targeting for your client and expected results.

Set Up a Facebook Business Manager Account:

If you don't have one yet, you can sign up to get an account on Facebook Business Manager account. It will serve as the central point for management of advertisements and other assets of the client.

To make it easier to manage your ad connect the Business Manager with the client's Facebook Page as well as an ad account.

Create an Ad Campaign:

Create a new ad campaign using the Ads Manager for a start. Pick a purpose for your campaign like the generation of leads, brand recognition or conversions that matches your customer's goals for advertising.

Based on variables like geography, demographics as well as interests, behaviors and connections, determine the intended audience. In order to find the ideal group, Facebook provides a variety of options for targeting.

Develop Compelling Ad Creative:

Facebook users are drawn to designs with a unique style which are appealing visually. For increased engagement of users make use of compelling content appealing images and videos as well as compelling calls to take action.

Ensure that the design of the advertisement is in line with the branding and identity of your client's messages.

Set Ad Placements and Budget:

Based on the goals and the target audience of your company, you can choose your best advertising placements. The options of Facebook include the community network, the messenger news feed, as well as stories.

Make a budget to finance the Facebook advertisement campaign for your customer. In determining your budget, consider the length of the campaign, how many people are involved and the expected outcomes.

Select Bidding Strategy:

Select a bidding method which is compatible with the goals and budgetary constraints of your customer. Cost per click (CPC) as well as cost per 1,000 impressions (CPM) and cost per step (CPA) are all options on Facebook.

Optimise your bid strategy based on the objectives and outcomes that the campaign has produced.

Monitor, Optimise, and Test:

Monitor the efficiency of your client's Facebook ads frequently. Check important metrics, such as the number of impressions, reach and engagement rates, click-throughs and conversions.

Choose the those areas where you need to improve and then implement improvements based on data. This could involve altering the target, the bid strategy or advertising locations.

Track Conversions and Pixel Integration:

On behalf of your clients' website you can install Facebook Pixel to track conversions and enhance ad performance in relation to the user's behavior.

Conversion tracking can be used to determine the efficiency of advertising campaigns for your clients as well as retarget those who already expressed an curiosity about their goods or products or.

Reporting and Client Communication:

Create detailed reports that show how your client's Facebook ads performed. In the report, highlight significant information, conclusions and recommendations for the upcoming ads.

Be in contact with your customers frequently and with a clear manner. Let them know about the state of their campaigns, the results, and any improvements of your Facebook advertising campaigns.

It is possible to leverage Facebook's huge audience and advanced targeted features for your benefit when you set up ads for your clients on the platform to generate impressive results for customers. In order to create successful campaigns, be familiar with Facebook's advertising tools, rules as well as best practices. To maximize the ROI You must constantly monitor your progress, adjust, and then report on the results of their Facebook marketing campaigns.

Setting Up the Reactivation Campaign

Reactivation campaigns can be a great means of reconnecting with previous customers or clients who expressed an interest in your company's products or services, but abandoned the services. In this chapter, we will look at how to organize a reactivation program to the benefit of your SMMA (Social Media Marketing Agency) in this section. It is possible to rekindle the interest of your customer base improve conversion rates, and increase the value of a customer's lifetime by running the right reactivation plan.

Identify Inactive Customers:

With your customer identify the proportion of their client base who have stopped engaging. It can be determined through factors like previous purchases emails, past purchases, or the activity on their website.

Find out what specific requirements your company's client utilizes to define the term "inactive" client.

Define Campaign Goals:

Set clear goals for your reactivation strategy in conjunction with your client. The goals could be to increase the level of customer engagement, increasing repeat businesses, or boosting the brand's loyalty.

Ensure that the goals of your campaign align with your client's primary business goals.

Segment the Inactive Customer List:

Based on similar characteristics or patterns of behavior You can segment your customer list that is inactive. The messages and offers you send out are able to be customized according to the segment you are targeting by segmentation that will increase the efficiency of your campaign.

Segments are determined using factors like previous purchases, demographics or specific product preferences.

Craft Compelling Messaging:

Create unique and compelling messages to reach out to each customers segment. Focus on their unique problems, offer discounts or rewards, and emphasize the advantages to get them involved in the business of your client.

To prompt immediate action, convey the message a feeling of urgency or exclusiveness.

Choose Communication Channels:

In order to reach out to your less active clients, select the most effective ways to communicate with them. It could be a personalised direct mail or social media channels, sending out SMS messages, or even email marketing.

When selecting the channel you will use, be sure to consider the habits and routines of your intended group of viewers.

Design Engaging Content:

For a reactivation strategy Create attractive and appealing contents. This could be in for example appealing photos on social media, appealing emails, or even specially made offers specifically for each segment.

Utilize user-generated content reviews, or stories to draw attention to the brand of your customer and trigger intense emotional responses.

Implement Automation:

For making the reactivation process more effective, you can use the tools for marketing automation. Develop automated procedures that can deliver personalised emails in response to specific actions of customers or actions.

To guarantee prompt and efficient outreach, automate the sending of messages via email, social media advertisements and other messages.

Track and Measure Results:

Utilize tracking software to assess the effectiveness of your reactivation campaigns. For tracking important metrics such as open rates, click-through rate as well as conversions and Reactivation rates, create reports and analytics tools.

Take data-driven decision making for future reactivation campaigns by analyzing data in order to identify trends, optimize your campaign and discover patterns.

Continuous Optimization:

Continuously adjust your reactivation strategy in accordance with the results that you have gathered. For the most effective strategies to engage your non-active clients, try various messaging options or offers as well as ways to distribute your message.

To enhance your general customer experience, you can modify your marketing campaign in response to customer feedback and interaction.

Evaluate and Iterate:

Results of the reactivation campaigns must be evaluated regularly The results must be communicated to your customer. Provide suggestions and feedback for regular customer reactivation strategies.

Based on the feedback of your clients and on the evolving requirements of their customers Iterate and refine the strategy you are using.

Re-engage with inactive clients and maximizing the potential of their earnings Your client will get significant outcomes by using the reactivation program. For the most effective outcomes, tailor your messages make use of automation and constantly improve your campaigns.

Setting up appointment Booking and Automations To manage customer appointments and improve the process of managing client appointments and streamline your SMMA (Social Media Marketing Agency) operation, effective appointment scheduling and automating processes are vital. In this chapter, we will discuss the steps to establish appointments scheduling systems as well as putting automatizations in place to improve the efficiency of your business and boost client service.

Choose an Appointment Booking System:

Select a reliable appointment-scheduling system that is based on the information you have gathered and your clients as well as agency's needs. Take into consideration things like price and customization options, as well as the possibility of integration and the ease of use.

Calendly Acuity Scheduling, Bookafy, and numerous other popular programs for scheduling appointments are readily available.

Set Up Your Booking System:

Create a profile on your company and then sign up for appointment booking services you prefer. Create options for the length of your appointment as well as buffer time between appointments and the times that are available.

To ensure availability of appointments and avoid booking doubles, incorporate the booking system into your calendar (such like Google Calendar).

Define Appointment Types and Availability:

Pick the types of appointments you'll be offering, including strategic meetings, calls for consultation or reviews of campaign results. Provide details about the time and purpose of each kind of appointment.

Based on your current working schedule, the demands of clients, and availability of your team, you can set the time you'd like to be available.

Chapter 7: Creating The Booking Script For Your Niche

It is essential to create an effective booking plan specific to your specific niche in order to connect to potential clients effectively and make leads turn into scheduled appointment. This chapter will explain the steps to create a booking script specifically for you SMMA (Social Media Marketing Agency) business. This will guide the conversations you have with potentlal clients to ensure that your messages are consistent as well as increase your chances of securing appointments.

Understand Your Niche:

Get a deep knowledge of your area and specific challenges, issues and goals of firms that work in it. Examine trends in the market, typical challenges in marketing, and strategy for success.

Learn the language as well as the terms and aspects that are specific to your field.

Define Your Value Proposition:

Find out what benefits that your business can provide clients within your field. Determine your competitive advantages and ways in which your offerings will meet the specific needs and needs of firms within your field.

Create a compelling value proposition that highlights the benefits and outcomes from the partnership with your agency can offer your clients.

Outline the Booking Call Structure:

The script for your booking call should be arranged in a way that flows effectively. Write down the main elements of your call which include introduction, qualification, the value proposition, how to handle objections, and finally closing.

Each section should serve a purpose that is clear and bring the prospective client just one more step towards arranging an appointment.

Introduce Yourself and Your Agency:

introduce yourself and your firm and the knowledge you have gained from your field in the first part of the conference call. Through focusing on successful niche-specific marketing programs or customer testimonials You can build credibility and confidence.

Be sure to highlight the unique value your company provides to businesses that are in your industry.

Qualify the Prospect:

To assess the potential customer and determine their specific demands and needs, pose specific questions. Know about the company's mission and goals, the budget and the desired outcomes.

You can adapt your strategy according to responses from the prospective customer in order to prove that you're conscious of their unique situations.

Present Your Value Proposition:

Please describe how you assist the prospective client's problems and objectives through addressing their needs within your agency's proposition of value. Provide relevant cases studies or stories of success and emphasize the benefits that you've achieved for your clients within the field.

Choose words that convey the particular challenges and objectives of the prospective client.

Handle Objections:

Prepare convincing arguments to the common concerns that potential customers could raise. Discuss issues related to financial restrictions or rivalries, past failures or even skepticism.

Overcome objections with solid proof, references or solutions tailored to the requirements of the prospective client.

Offer the Appointment:

When you've resolved all concerns and demonstrated the value of your company make sure you invite the prospect to meet with a representative in order to explore the prospective client's needs in marketing. It is important to clearly explain your purpose and benefits and present it as a great opportunity to discuss the strategies that they can use for their business.

Offer the prospective client options to make an appointment, taking into consideration their availability and preferred method for contact.

Handle Logistics and Confirm Details:

Organize the logistics including confirming the meeting's date or time as well as venue. The prospect should be given specific instructions regarding how they can prepare for the appointment, as well as any other documents or information they'll need.

Check your prospect's contacts twice to ensure a seamless communications.

Follow Up and Nurture:

Make sure to send a follow-up email or message as quickly as you can to thank the person who made the appointment for their time and reiterate the significance of the scheduled appointment. Additional information or sources are to be provided to the prospect.

Keep the connection going by staying in touch, and delivering relevant information including content and invites to webinars and other events.

It is possible to effectively interact with potential customers, respond to the concerns of their customers, and set up lucrative appointments with an efficient booking plan for your particular niche. You can constantly modify your script in response to feedback from your prospects as well as the evolving requirements of your industry. Be aware that the success of your SMMA is contingent on your capacity to learn from mistakes and adapt.

Creating Your Launch Call Presentation

In a sales meeting, an introduction to the call is a crucial tool to providing clear information about the advantages as well as the strategies and solutions provided by your business for prospective clients. In this section we'll explore the steps to create an introduction to your launch event that can grab the audience's focus and make them select you as your SMMA (Social Media Marketing Agency) to fulfill their needs in marketing.

Define the Purpose and Structure:

Take a final decision on the purpose of your launch presentation. Do you want to educate potential customers about your services or highlight your expertise or provide a brief description of the services that you provide? Set clear objectives to guide the creation of content.

Organise your presentation in a systematic manner and efficiently, while ensuring an effortless transition between sections and the next.

Introduction and Agency Overview:

Make sure to begin with a captivating opening to entice the attention of your viewers. Indicate your business' name, mission as well as your special offer for clients.

To build credibility and build confidence, provide a concise description of your organization's background of experience, expertise, and research studies.

Understand Prospect's Needs:

Prior to the call for launch make some study and determine the individual needs issues, goals and challenges. It is important to highlight your unique goals and challenges when you present your message.

If you make references to their competitors, industry and current marketing techniques it is possible to prove you've done your homework.

Present Services and Strategies:

Highlight the range of the services you offer and the way they can fulfill the requirements of your potential customer. Provide a detailed explanation of each one, and focus on the benefits and effects they are likely to see.

Show your expertise in the various platforms for social media including marketing techniques, the creation of content, analytics or any other topics which are relevant.

Provide Examples and Case Studies:

Provide concrete examples and examples that demonstrate the way your strategies for promoting your business work in real-world situations. In order to demonstrate the benefits your service has produced for previous customers Utilize numbers, metrics as well as testimonials.

To demonstrate the credibility and relevance of your message, focus on successful stories that are from the potential client's business sector or related sectors.

Address Common Concerns:

Examine possible objections or concerns that are common and then respond to the concerns. Price, ROI competition, perceived risk are just a few of the examples.

Write reassuring and calming responses to alleviate their fears and emphasize the value of what your organization can provide.

Outline the Collaboration Process:

The step-by-step process in working with your agency. This includes the planning, execution and monitoring of campaign. For clear communication set out each person's role and duties.

It is important to emphasize your business's commitment towards collaboration, communicating, and the achievement of outcomes.

Offer Customised Solutions:

Provide specialized methods or solutions for your prospect's specific requirements during the presentation. An individual approach to tackle your prospects' challenges must be proved by showing you've given them a lot of consideration.

Display your skills through providing tips and advice which support their mission.

Visuals and Multimedia:

To improve comprehension and participation, incorporate interactive infographics, multimedia, and other visuals into your presentations. Utilize charts, graphs, or images that show before and after to demonstrate the ways in which your methods have proven successful.

It is important to ensure that the layout represents the image of the agency, and looks professional, neat, appealing to the eye.

Call to Action:

Create a powerful call to action near the conclusion of your talk. If you would like the prospective client to set up a follow-up phone meeting, or sign a contract or commence an initial trial, make certain to mention that when you make your demand.

It should be easy for prospective clients to reach you, and then continue to work with your agency, by giving contact details.

Make sure you practice the presentation to ensure that you're able to present the message confidently and convincingly. Adjust and revise the presentation for your launch depending on the feedback of your customers, trends in the market and the changing needs of buyers. The chances of turning potential customers into long-term customers of your SMMA can be significantly increased when you have a compelling and attractive presentation.

Watching SMMA Onboarding Process Videos

The owners of SMMAs (Social Media Marketing Agencies)--whether they're experienced or are just beginning their journey, they must continuously update their knowledge and stay on top of the current developments in business. In this article we'll look at what watching SMMA video tutorials on the process of onboarding can assist your business to grow and thrive.

Understanding the Onboarding Process:

This is the very first step in where you greet new customers and establish the foundation for a productive working relationship. This involves gathering client information as well as setting goals and co-ordinating expectations.

The videos that illustrate the SMMA onboarding process provide useful information about the onboarding process of clients by effective agencies.

Learning Best Practices:

Learn from experienced professionals as well as experts in the field when you watch the SMMA video tutorials on how to board. Learn about their best tips, techniques to successfully in boarding customers.

Know how to accelerate the process of onboarding Set clear expectations and encourage open communication.

Customising Your Onboarding Process:

Based on their targeted market, its services, and internal workflows, every SMMA is unique in its way of boarding its clients. It is possible to get ideas as well as inspiration to tailor your own process for onboarding through watching video clips showing the process of onboarding at work.

The strategies that are in line with your agency's goals, values and customer base must be modified before putting in practice.

Enhancing Client Experience:

A well-organized and structured onboarding process can create a favorable setting for a good client-agency interaction. Learn how improve the experience for clients in the process of onboarding by watching videos on the process of onboarding.

Learn to communicate with customers in an efficient way, address the clients' questions and concerns and provide a seamless entry to your services.

Avoiding Common Pitfalls:

Onboarding new clients is often a challenge and hazard-filled. Learn about common mistakes and traps to avoid in the process of onboarding through watching SMMA onboarding videos.

Find out strategies to control the expectations of clients, managing issues with scope creep, and insuring that your clients have a smooth integration into the services of your agency.

Incorporating New Tools and Technologies:

The field of marketing via digital channels is always shifting, and innovative tools as well as technologies are continually being created. Video clips about onboarding for customers frequently demonstrate the ways in which certain technologies and tools can be utilized.

Discover cutting-edge software, programs or other tools that accelerate and enhance the effectiveness of your onboarding process.

Maintaining Up-to-date with industry trends:

SMMA video tutorials on the process of onboarding will keep you updated on the most current changes and trends within the industry. Discover new strategies as well as new platforms and shifting expectations of customers in the SMMA sector.

Stay ahead of market by incorporating current trends as well as insights into the procedure for onboarding.

Chapter 8: Rinse And Repeat

1:Using Leadsie for Client Ad Account Access

It is essential to put in place efficient procedures in order to access and managing clients' advertising accounts when you run successful SMMA (Social Media Marketing Agency). The process can be simplified by using Leadsie and also provides secured access to the client's ad accounts. In this chapter, we will discuss the benefits Leadsie can offer your business along with how you can utilize it to access client advertising accounts.

Understanding Leadsie:

It is a service specifically designed for agencies that allow quick and secure access to clients advertising accounts. It functions as a connection between your agency and customers, making the connecting and management of advertising accounts much easier.

With the central dashboard of Leadsie it is possible to manage the view and edit of advertisements on a variety of platforms.

Benefits of Using Leadsie:

Secure Access to Accounts: Leadsie uses stringent authentication processes to protect the security of ad account accounts for clients. For security of sensitive data the company uses access control systems as well as secure connections.

Increased Efficiency: When making use of Leadsie the user can avoid making ads accounts manually and transferring login credentials with your clients. To help reduce time and energy and time, the software provides a simple way to access client ads accounts.

Integrated Dashboard with Leadsie the ability to connect to and management of multiple advertising accounts of your clients via a single, easy-to-use screen. Thus, your campaigns are more organized and monitored. This results in a more efficient work flow.

Transparency and Collaboration: Leadsie encourages client and agency cooperation. The company gives customers access to the information they need on their marketing campaigns which allows them to measure the effectiveness of their campaigns and monitor the evolution of their marketing strategies.

Starting with Leadsie:

Create an account and sign up configuration: Sign up for an account with Leadsie account and then complete the initial setup procedures. Connecting your current ads accounts as well as providing the some basic information about your agency.

"Client Onboarding": Ask your clients to join to their Leadsie advertising accounts. Send them clear directions about how they can proceed, and assure them of the benefits of the platform as well as its safety.

The account authorization process: Once they have opening their accounts for advertising the clients have to give your agency access to and control the campaigns. The agency will guide them by Leadsie throughout the authorization process to ensure a smooth procedure.

Accessing and Managing Client Ad Accounts:

You are able to access the ad accounts of your clients by using the Leadsie dashboard after they have agreed to allow you to do this. You can then observe the outcomes by analyzing results of campaigns, making modifications as well as launching new campaigns.

Use Leadsie's features as well as tools to generate reports for your clients. keep track of important metrics, and optimize your campaigns.

Communication and Reporting:

Use the communication tools offered by Leadsie to ensure that your relationships with clients flexible and productive. Utilize the forums to share details, discuss tactics as well as answer questions or issues.

Create detailed reports with Leadsie for your clients. These reports will provide them with complete information regarding campaign efficiency and return on investment and other vital indicators.

Ongoing Maintenance and Support:

Malntain your Leadsie account on a regular basis and ensure sure that the ad accounts of your clients' accounts are accessible and connected. For the best experience of Leadsie make sure you are informed of any changes or brand new features made available.

Contact Leadsie's customer support department in case you encounter issues or are having questions concerning the platform. They will be able to provide support as well as direction so that everything runs without a hitch.

It is possible to speed up the process of onboarding clients, enhance security and run campaigns across different platforms using Leadsie for account access to clients. access. Make use of this powerful device to improve the efficiency of your company, promote clients to collaborate, and lead successful marketing campaigns.

Using Uphex for 1-click Ad Uploads

One of the most important aspects to running successful SMMA (Social Media Marketing Agency) is efficiently managing and uploading ads on various platforms. Utilizing the powerful software Uphex the process of uploading advertisements is simplified, thereby saving time while streamlining the process. In this chapter, we will discuss the benefits Uphex provides your business and how you can make use of it to perform 1-click uploads.

Understanding Uphex:

An extensive platform known as Uphex was developed for making it simpler to post ads to social media platforms such as Facebook,

Instagram, Twitter and LinkedIn. It offers a simple user interface with powerful automation capabilities that make the process of the process of managing and running ads easier.

Through Uphex's simple advertising upload feature that allows you to easily and rapidly upload campaigns across multiple platforms all at the same time.

Benefits of Using Uphex:

Efficiency in Time Uploading ads requires a fraction of the time and effort because of Uphex. With Uphex, it is possible for users to design and publish ads to each platform fast and effortlessly, saving time as well as money.

A streamlined workflow: by making use of Uphex allows you to streamline the process of managing campaigns. Uphex provides an integrated dashboard on which it is possible to oversee multiple marketing campaigns, evaluate their results, and make changes.

Uphex offers automation tools that ensure consistency across your advertising campaigns. There are predefined guidelines and templates in order to be sure your advertisements conform to all the requirements required and the branding guidelines of your company.

Improved Accuracy: Uphex reduces the possibility of error by humans while uploading adverts. A lot of manual work is made automated by the platform that reduces the chance of mistakes and assures a accurate campaign execution.

Support for various platform: Uphex is compatible with well-known social media platforms. This allows users to post ads to several networks at the same time. This will increase the reach of your ads and helps you control campaigns across different platforms.

Starting with Uphex:

Create an Uphex account and then complete the initial setup process. Connect your social media ads accounts with Uphex and provide the required agency details.

Development of Ad Templates: For consistent branding and messages across your campaigns create ad templates within Uphex. These templates can be customized to suit the specific requirements of every platform.

Configuring Up campaign settings: When you are in Uphex, you can set the campaign's settings, such as targets, budget allocation and schedule. In the process of uploading this settings will be added to the campaign.

Uploading ads using Uphex

Selecting Campaigns: From the Uphex dashboard, pick your campaigns to publish. Pick the advertising groups or sets that you would like to share across multiple platforms.

Pick your preferred social media platform and then enter the URLs for the ads you wish to display there. It is possible to select multiple platforms using Uphex all at once which eliminates the burden of uploading each campaign one at a to each of the platforms.

Review and affirm before you begin the upload make sure you double-check the platform and campaigns that you've picked. Verify that the necessary template and settings are present.

One-Click Upload Uphex initiates the uploading of advertisements to platforms of your choice by just one click. It handles all technical aspect, ensuring that campaigns are put in place in a correct manner.

Monitoring and Optimization:

Make use of Uphex's reporting and analytics tools to measure the performance of your marketing campaigns. Examine important metrics such as impressions and clicks, as well as conversions and ROI to see the extent to which your advertising campaigns work.

Based on your data on performance, you can adjust and optimize Uphex according to the need. This increases the effectiveness of campaigns and yields better results for you clients.

Support and Updates:

In case of any difficulties or queries you need to address when using the platform, Uphex is available for support on a regular basis. To get assistance or help with troubleshooting Contact their customer support.

Stay up to date with Uphex's latest enhancements and features. Utilize the latest features to help you manage your marketing campaigns.

It is possible to reduce time, increase efficiency and assure the same campaign's deployment across all social media platforms using the Uphex tool for one-click advertisement uploads. Make use of this powerful device to improve the process of managing your campaigns and create effective marketing campaigns for your customers.

Chapter 9: Social Media Marketing For Businesses

Social media marketing can be an effective way that all businesses to engage with clients and potential customers. In reality, your clients are likely already communicating with other brands on the most popular social media platforms. Thus, you must be interacting with your clients, putting up content and engaging with them on these social networks in order to avoid losing out.

A few of the most well-known social media sites are Instagram, Pinterest, Twitter, YouTube, Facebook, and Google. If you own an online company, you should make sure to get your business on one or more of these sites. Social media has the potential to provide you with a remarkable boost in sales and provide you with loyal customers. It is also possible to manage additional issues via social media, such as selling, customer services etc.

What is Social Media Marketing?

Social media marketing can be described as a type of marketing strategy that is based on the internet. It is the process of creating media content, and sharing it through social media sites with your people who are followers, friends, and with the large public. There are millions of users on social media around the globe. Inviting them to join your company by using social media is what social media marketing all about.

The most common tasks associated with social media marketing are posting relevant videos, uploading writing articles, or updating photos. All of these are posted so that you can entice your readers, viewers, and your followers. If you interact with the audience, address their concerns or respond to their remarks You gain trust and they start to believe on your credibility. In order to increase engagement with your customers and place ads that are paid for are important components of social media marketing.

Strategies for marketing small-scale companies

Many small-scale business owners are careful how much they spend. They take care when choosing their marketing tactics that they are investing in mainly since they are on a tight budget and desire to make maximum value out of their investment as they can.

It is recommended for an owner of a small-sized business to make wise investments to maximize the return. One of the best methods of making this happen is using social media channels. This type of strategy can be used in a variety of ways with low-cost strategies that are actually effective. There is no surprise that nearly 97% of marketing professionals use social media since many of their customers and prospective customers are on some or all of these social media platforms.

Your customers are already on social media

One reason why you must promote your company is because your clients are using social media platforms and spend a significant amount of time on it each all day. Based on reliable data that over 70 percent of US citizens are on some social media site or another. The amount of users on social media around the globe could grow to 2.5 billion in the coming year. Because so many users are connected to social media, it is logical to send messages to the users. Small-scale businesses are provided with the opportunity to engage with an enormous audience.

The consumer is more responsive via social media

It's been proven that users are more accepting of messages from marketers on social media than other channels. It is due to the fact that social networks provide an exciting and enjoyable opportunity to network, interact and remain in contact with family and friends. Though users may not use social networks to receive promotional communications from business but they do respond particularly when they are approached by engaging and fun approach. The majority of users on social media like to engage with their favourite brands.

The brand name is recognized on social media

One of the primary advantages that social media has is that it assists small businesses increase the exposure of their brand and their products. As visibility improves your company's brand is recognized and appreciation from your customers as well as your followers. It is essential to establish business social media profiles on various platforms since they can provide new opportunities and fresh and thrilling possibilities. It allows you to publish the content you create and show off your company's voice and personality.

Make sure that you publish interesting information, such as videos, articles or photos that bring worth to the customers. In this way, you'll be making sure that your name is easily accessible to customers and that they know about the brand. For instance, think about a user on the internet that comes across your content. The user may not know about your business and/or brand, however your content could be intriguing enough. In the end, this user may find your service appealing and might even recommend it to his circle of 200 to 500 of his friends and fans.

Build Your Own Personal Brand

If you post content on the internet it gives you the chance to build an online character. The persona you create reflects your skills and abilities as a professional and personal beliefs. Most business owners use social media for the purpose of putting on display their brand and services. A lot of others make connections, vital leads as well as loyal followers and clients.

Below are a few tips you should follow to build your brand and make it more visible through social media. In doing this you can grow your following and reach get the attention of your customers and build a massive following in an extremely short period of duration.

1. Make sure to select and change your social network of choice

There are many social media sites available. It is important to select one or two of the most significant ones, based on factors like preferences and more. When you've chosen your top social media account You should make them up-to-date with your company's names, addresses, and brands as well as adding any content you want to add. If you've any existing accounts you no longer using, either close them or erase them.

It is vital to make sure that your existing accounts are updated with current content and correct data. In this way, you'll increase visitors to the social networks pages which you would like to promote. This also gives you the opportunity to delete all content that is inappropriate or unnecessary which does not speak well about your personal image.

2. Make sure to share your content frequently

It is recommended that you are sharing pertinent and interesting content with your fans on a regular on a regular basis. It is essential discern between sharing interesting and pertinent content versus posting unrelated posts, and excessive posting. When you publish too many occasions, followers may find it uninteresting and unprofessional. Your goal is to keep them active and keep the contact lines open. But, sharing too much can make appear unkempt and unprofessional. It is best to post at least 3-4 times per week and responding to queries, comments and queries regarding your postings.

According to experts the fact that posting a single message on social media is not going to make a difference in the results. That's why it's recommended to publish posts on various social media sites at least once per week. In the case of Instagram, for instance, you could publish 3-4 occasions each day on Facebook, Instagram, and Twitter Then follow-up on the posts with comments on the posts and replies to remarks.

3. Produce and distribute content

It is also important to make your own content or, if you prefer, curate content you are interested in. Make sure to share these with your followers, and let them know how easy it is to share the content with other people or leave remarks.

4. Transfer your contacts

There are probably plenty of people on different platforms. One of the most reliable sources for contacts that are useful are the contacts you have in your email account and your address book. Beginning with well-known sites such as Outlook and Gmail before moving to your phone book. Then, you can check out other platforms on the internet like LinkedIn, Facebook, Instagram and many more. In this way, you can quickly build up a follower base in no time. They will eventually be able to have their own followers. In addition, the multiplier effect will mean that you'll get additional followers.

5. Be positive and always keep your focus on the positive.

On social media sites, be sure to present the most positive side of yourself every time. An excellent social image is appealing and can make others want to follow you. There are several aspects you should take care of to keep your image as positive and your company. The social media channels you use must always be considered a reflection of your personal style and professionalism.

You must refrain from being argumentative, and keep clear of any racist or controversial religious statements. Additionally, you should be extremely cautious when you post remarks about politics because people may not agree with you or, worse yet might be offended by the comments you make. If it comes down to it, you should you should consider establishing two separate accounts on social media, where one is personal, and the other is designed specifically for your company and company.

6. Make sure to join a couple of different groups

The best way to succeed and develop in social media is to join groups. The social media sites like Facebook as well as LinkedIn offer a variety of groups that members can join. To locate a group that is similar to yours make use of the search feature located on the top of every social media. After you have joined a certain group, you are able to interact with the group members, and also post interesting content you discover among your fans. There are no advantages if you join the group only to become inactive. Think about becoming an active member as you participate in the discussions and debates. Offer your personal views and perspectives on the topics being debated, and then share this to your friends and followers.

Product Launch on Social Media

The days and weeks that lead up to a launch could be very chaotic and thrilling all at once. The most vital element of a successful launch is getting information out. Consider a tree that is in the forest. Can it be heard even if there is no one around? Similar questions apply to new product launches. This is the point where social platforms can be useful. Social media platforms help get the message out.

The advent of social media has completely changed the way that advertising is conducted. When properly used it can assist in the promotion of a particular company's sales. Sites such as Facebook as well as Instagram can be great for launching new products. There are a number of reasons for why these launch campaigns are successful, and it's important these factors are recognized.

Make sure you are prepared

A different aspect that is crucial to an event is the creation of anticipation. This involves dropping hints or posting pictures of products, and generally generating excitement about the announcement. The result is unintended buzz on various platforms and a large number of people can get the stage for discussion about the launch date and your company and your products. It is essential to take care when launching any anticlimax releases as they are likely to harm your business. Be sure that you're able to meet the market once the product is launched.

Word spoken through mouth

One of the most efficient method of getting word out about the product is via the power of word-of-mouth. Social media websites benefit from this and aid in getting the message out across to millions of users. If you are a business owner who operates online must make sure you are strategic in your strategy.

Begin with the appropriate wording and then strategically place it. If executed correctly the social media marketing campaign could help you reach an enormous audience that will be delighted to hear about it. One of the main aspects of this procedure is to allow others on social media platforms be aware of the excitement and excitement, and then help propagate the news.

Sit back and observe as people adopt the cause and pass the word on through their networks. Some will also share the campaign on different networks, and in short time, the feedback begin to come into. It's also recommended to get in touch with influencers, and allow them to test your product to find out what they are saying about it.

To attract early adopters

It is advisable to bring the early adopters to your brand. Products that are technologically advanced appeal to these types of people. They really want to be first to try an innovative product that is on the market, and later post reviews on blogs and social media.

If you can attract early users, they'll quickly turn into your advertising champions ahead of schedule. It is important to allow influential people a look at your products and then let them share the details to their millions of fans on social media and followers. This can create an exciting buzz and create excitement in on the market, making them keen to purchase and utilize your product.

How to target your market

One benefit that social media has is the fact that you can set up ways to concentrate on certain segments in the marketplace. The fact is that the vast majority of social media users have a range of ages from 18 and 35. This group of people is hugely important in determining the effectiveness of a newly released product.

There is also the possibility to make use of social media platforms to market other areas of the market such as older generation. Though a large portion is not on social networks, the use of influential young people and the younger population to promote a product can in the end have a massive influence on older generations. This strategy is far more effective than conventional product launches.

Social Media Marketing and Small Businesses and Franchises

One of the many benefits from social media is the fact that it has created a level playing field so that the smaller companies can be competitive with their larger counterparts.

Small-scale businesses are always searching for innovative and successful strategies to get their company and their brand known in order for potential clients to locate them. If you're not employing social media, you're missing out significantly. Social media can be beneficial for business because it offers you opportunities to gain new customers and engage with existing customers frequently.

In reality small-sized businesses enjoy an advantage over larger companies when it comes to marketing via social media. For this reason, for your social media marketing to be successful the business must interact with customers, followers as well as people in general. If a company does not communicate with customers and its followers won't be able to achieve success through social media.

Social media and small businesses

Engaging with customers via social media is an essential marketing tactic for any business but is especially important for small ones. According to research that found over 90 percent of marketing professionals said that they use social media in their jobs. The majority of them are employed by small-sized businesses. In order to be successful in social media, even as a tiny business owner, you must create a plan to regularly engage with your customers.

How to Use Social Media for Franchises and Social Media

1. Be cautious and start with a small approach: If you're a company manager looking to draw new clients and build a large followership, you may be enticed to create accounts on the most popular social media platforms. You should however, avoid this method. Make sure you only open one account on social media and concentrate on it for a time. After you've learned the basics can you go on by opening new accounts on other platforms.

2. Start your own blog One of the best ways to help the marketing of your social media is the blog. If you have already an existing website, then establishing the blog is straightforward. It is recommended to set up an additional website to host your blog.

A blog can be a wonderful place to write captivating content that you and then share with your friends via your social media profiles. Readers are also able to share content through their social media pages using buttons for sharing.

It is essential to write engaging and informative posts for your blog as well as your social media accounts. Content marketing is a fascinating innovative tool that is widely utilized by corporations to advertise their brand and product. It is the reason why content is essential. It is essential to be engaging your followers regularly by providing them with interesting and exciting information. The kind of interactions you provide to your followers is sure to keep them interested and committed to your business.

3. Make a calendar of your content: It's an excellent idea to organize your content to ensure that your interactions with social media platforms are consistent and well-coordinated, not random and sudden. Try to schedule your social media engagements at least a month ahead. While you're waiting you are able to look through different social media sites or networks for content that you can send to your followers. Make sure to engage them at least four times per week or so.

Make sure you don't post regularly as it can be viewed as spammy and irritating. Keep in mind that certain seasons during the calendar are attractive to customers, which includes those who follow you. This includes those of the New Year, the start of spring and summer, Memorial Day, holiday time, Thanksgiving, and many more. Make the most of the holidays in order to raise your awareness of your brand and perhaps even increase sales.

4. Spend the time to develop an audience. It requires some time and energy to create a decent audience in social networks. A majority of your followers will only be following you when you invite them directly. Thus, it is important to locate followers and create an following. Your followers anticipate receiving fresh and interesting content every 3-4 days from your side. It will take approximately six months to get your customers to believe in you and to begin buying your goods. Within that period they'll be sharing the content they have to their

followers and networks as well as harass you with queries regarding your product.

5. Assess your progress: When you begin to build a significant followers on social media sites that converts into leads and sales, then you need to begin evaluating the efficacy and effectiveness of your work. The most important thing to be doing is tracking the outcomes to determine the percentage of new clients are coming via social media websites. If they're engaging with social media sites, you must connect with them to learn more regarding their activities. Monitoring the effectiveness of your social networks is crucial to your business's success.

6. Find out more about advertising prior to spending money on it It is sometimes essential to promote your business via social media. It is recommended to pay for ads however, don't immediately dive into the process. It is better to understand the basics of the social media marketing. Be sure to first ensure that you are able to attract a large fan

base before you can place ads. If you just jump in to advertisements without careful planning and thought, you're more likely to fail and lose the money.

Reasons Why Small Businesses are More Successful on Social Media

1. They're more focused at the individuals and communities The vast difference between small companies as well as large companies. In particular, big companies are staffed by huge numbers of workers with numerous legal and administrative structure, with the majority of decisions implemented at the corporate headquarters which are many miles further away. But, there are a few variations that are important.

In particular, small-scale businesses tend to be more focused on the individual and their communities. They hire locally, they sell locally and make sure that their earnings stay within the community. In this way, they're in a position to connect easily to their clients. Smaller businesses are more able to engage and communicate with their customers and followers via the web. If you are a small-sized business owner it is easy to manage your comments as well as other posts on your social media accounts. So make sure you reply to as many of the comments as you are able to.

Social media can be a fantastic way for consumers to talk about various items and services. Remember to welcome responses, feedback, inquiries or concerns and any other communications from clients. Making connections with customers is easy for smaller entrepreneurs, but a bit more difficult for larger businesses. Customers, whether prospective or actual, will display greater gratitude for those who respond quickly to feedback and express their concerns, views, and points of view.

2. Advertising on social media is extremely efficient in terms of cost: Traditional advertising can be costly. It is however, a lot different when it comes to social media since

cost is almost negligible. It's possible to run the entire process from start through sales with no large amount. Social media is home to many millions of active users, so the ability to connect with this large population at less than the expense for traditional advertisements is remarkable. Even if you choose to put some money into real-time advertising on social networks it will allow you choose your audience and costs will be minimal and cost-effective.

Social media marketing is an effective tool for business particularly small-sized businesses in order to reach out to clients and to increase the amount of sales. Send out regular news to customers as well as fans, informing them about the latest merchandise, sales, or special offers.

Social media allows you to are not just able to market the current customers, but to prospective customers. It helps to put your business name noticed and allow all those interested to know more about the services you provide. Customers and your general audience are then your most important brand ambassadors as well as promoters.

3. Social media marketing initiatives that are joint Smaller businesses may collaborate via social media platforms to launch collective marketing campaigns. The two companies work together so that they can put their resources into similar strategies on social media for marketing. It can be a great option for local businesses to join forces with other companies in the same area and send out messages to those who are in the same area. Remember that these aren't competitors, but rather companies that have the same desires and operate in the same vicinity.

In this case, for example it is possible to announce that customers who purchase the products you sell will be given an offer that gives them an offer at a nearby retailer. One option would be to join forces with a local establishment and offer discount coupons and other giveaways. Contests are also popular, with winners receiving a prize from the participating businesses. If you partner with companies from other industries and organizations, you are increasing brand awareness as well as informing your followers and customers to purchase from other companies. It also draws more buyers to your shop.

4. Customer care that is personalized Smaller businesses like paying focus to their clients. A lot of consumers feel that buying from a small-scale business offers them an exceptional shopping experience. Actually, the large majority of people prefer shopping at small-scale stores due to the personal attention they receive. If you are a business proprietor it is your responsibility to take the time to communicate to your customers individually.

Attention to the fact that personal care should not be restricted to those who shop in stores just. The same should apply to those who purchase from your store online. Be sure to engage with your customers through social media on a personalized basis and do not use scripted responses that belong to huge corporates. They sell their products across the nation and are able to take the time and resources to offer personal responses to their customers. Small firms gain the edge. They can write authentic responses to your customers and take care to address their unique needs. This can give you and smaller businesses an obvious benefit in marketing.

5. Smaller businesses are able to take advantage of advertising that is big: There are some major event for advertising and marketing that take place often. Smaller companies can incorporate these occasions into their strategies for social marketing. For instance, consider for instance the Small Business Saturday or SBS. The day is dedicated to celebrating and encourage small-scale businesses throughout America. The event is held on the Sunday following Thanksgiving. As a large percentage of customers know about this holiday and you

could benefit through promoting your goods and perhaps offering discounts so that customers are motivated to buy your items or avail your services. This provides you with a huge possibility to increase customer base and generate profits.

Be sure to keep your branding and your business's name the same across all social media platforms. This allows people on social media to quickly locate your profile. That means that your existing as well as potential customers will identify them, while they will also be able to know more about your company as well as your offerings.

Why Do People Fail at Social Media Marketing?

You are aware that being active on social media is vital to your advertising and marketing campaigns. Also, you know that having a the presence of social media is crucial to your success overall as an enterprise. Research shows that 7 out of 10 Americans use social media. Therefore, engaging with them through these channels is vitally important.

In the realm of the social media world, entrepreneurs should be aware that there's plenty to be learned. There are many various social media platforms which is why it's crucial you choose the two or three sites essential to your marketing campaigns. It is essential to understand the guidelines if you wish to succeed and gain advantages over competitors. It is common for small-scale business owners to have a lot of mistakes to make with their social media marketing campaigns. making it hard to gain any progress. Below are the reasons individuals fail on the social media advertising strategies.

1. Tendencies against social media: The principal goal that social media has is to offer an opportunity for people to chat, talk or share their thoughts, ideas or interact with each other and exchange ideas. Some businesses choose to not communicate with their fans in any way. This could be like having

an event for the press and not answering any questions afterwards. It is essential that you are engaging your followers as well as your customers via your social media channels. Make sure you answer their queries, responding to their posts and sharing their tweets, and in general being active and social.

2. The key performance indicators have been left out If you are a business manager it is important to learn to set measurable goals. This goes for all areas of your company, it's not just about social media. There are many people in the marketing industry aren't completely sure of what important performance indicators to look for. They are of the opinion that re-tweets, likes as well as shares and follows are accurate indicators.

It's even more essential to set goals with measurable outcomes to measure the success of your advertising and marketing campaigns through social media. In this way, you'll know the best practices and avoid them. A few of these indicators are calls for directions, calls, etc.

3. Learn the nuances of various social networks. Sometimes, marketing professionals tend to treat each social network with the same manner using the same strategy for marketing and advertising their services. This is often referred to as a misinterpretation of culture as each social network differs. The right channels for advertising is crucial to the success of your advertising campaigns. It's as important as knowing where your ideal audience is. In other words, you may not have to join websites like Pinterest or Instagram for if you're a hosting service provider. If you run an establishment for baking, Instagram as well as Pinterest could be perfect for you.

4. Lack of content that is engaging The most important thing is to supply your audience with content of high quality which is interesting and pertinent. Content could be anything including video clips and photos to

text. It is essential that the content is pertinent appealing, engaging, memorable and enticing. By doing this, you will attract the audience to keep them entertained and will make them feel more comfortable with your brand, business, as well as your product. People are likely to leave feedback as well as ask questions or even ask for clarifications. If they do, you should not ignore them. Instead, you must interact with them, address your questions, comment their thoughts, and even like them and the list goes on. The personal touch is vital to the longevity of your company.

5. Lack of the necessary sources: Although social media can be largely cost-free to access, you require sufficient funds for your campaign to continue. Most entrepreneurs believe that they do not require anything since the platforms are totally free. However, there are assets to be able to execute effective campaigns. As an example, you'll have to own a site as well as you will also need a blog. It is also necessary to produce

content frequently, which includes pictures and videos. Without a budget chances are you'll fall short with your marketing initiatives. Before you do anything, it is essential sit down, think about and think about strategies for eventual successful outcomes.

6. Social media fear The fear of social media may be surprising, but the majority of people suffer from unanswered fears of websites that are social. This is actually one of the major reasons for the failure of businesses to use social media. The main reason for fearing the fear that they'll post things that are negative, which could damage their brand. However, not sharing is one of the most costly mistakes you could make. Making use of social media as a marketing tool and advertising is an extremely successful way to expand the business of your organization, boosting profits, as well as bringing in new customers.

Chapter 10: Which Is The Most Important Social Site?

Small businesses must be listed on two or more social media platforms. If you're not already and you're not, you're missing many opportunities. Social networks have a myriad of ways for you to use in order to communicate with customers. Consider the fact that more than 70 percent of Americans use social media or other. That means that your ads will reach out to a large population.

Social media enables people usually business owners, who are promoting their business, to reach certain groups of people. You can achieve this at incredibly low expenses while reaching a massive public. This low and reasonable cost that makes social media so popular for smaller companies. The cost of marketing affordable, but their coverage is considerably greater that is not the case for traditional marketing channels.

It is essential be aware that there are not all social media websites that will be suitable for all types of campaigns and all small business. There is a need to invest an hour or so learning about the many social media platforms available and the way they work. Spending the time to understand what each social media site does and how they operate will provide you with the edge over your competition and also benefits of coming up with best strategies, and also identifying your target audience.

Tops Social Media Websites for Businesses

1. Facebook: This website is a great choice for businesses of all sizes that want to increase exposure and engage with current and potential customers.

2. Instagram: This awe-inspiring social network is renowned for its video and images publishing. This is a great platform for companies who want to engage their customers via images and videos that mainly contains videos and images.

3. Twitter: Twitter is the perfect platform for companies that want to connect with a high-end and tech-savvy customer base through bite-sized content along with images and videos.

4. YouTube: This video-sharing site is great for B2C as well as B2B companies looking to deliver videos to their clients.

5. Pinterest It is a social media platform that is ideal for consumer-focused companies that are targeting specific segments like women.

6. Snapchat is the best social network for companies that are targeting teens and young adults who love to communicate in an entertaining way.

Factors Considered When Choosing Social Media for Business Purposes

1. Cost: A quality social media site should be free and must be totally cost-free. If you must pay for a subscription to social networks, you might not get value for money. There are

many websites that are free and popular to utilize.

2. The suitability of small-sized businesses Choose social networks with a effectiveness in small companies. Do not choose sites that have no track record.

3. Popularity: The majority of popular social media platforms have thousands of followers. Select those that have a huge follower base as they will provide an opportunity of being successful.

4. Usability Easy to use: The most popular social sites are the ones that are user-friendly for anyone to access.

5. Advanced features: You're capable of doing more and connect with clients and fans more effectively on social media networks using the latest tools.

6. Geographic targeting: The majority of small companies have a local area of operation, so having the capability to concentrate on a

certain segment within the industry or geographical area can add a lot of benefits.

7. Age-related: There exist social media platforms that are loved by specific age groups. As an example, Snapchat is popular among younger generations, whereas Facebook can be used by people from all ages.

This is a quick review of popular social media

Facebook

It is one of the most enduring and most widely used social media network currently that is currently in use. Facebook is incredibly well-known and has billions of people from across the globe. If you are a company there are a variety of options to select from such as opening professional profiles, creating specific ads, or paying for ads for promotion purposes.

Every company should be on Facebook because of its status. If used in the correct manner it could turn into a vital part of any company for marketing strategy, sales and customer service. Facebook is a great platform to share every kind of content between stories and images, to memes and videos.

When you sign up for a business account with us, you'll have access to a variety of powerful instruments that can help with your advertising and marketing campaigns. Additionally, you can avail numerous options for customization, allowing users to accomplish a range of goals, including highlighting the contact details including hours of operation, offerings of products or services along with your company's address.

Facebook is a great option for users who are of any age, even seniors. Many people older than 55 have Facebook accounts that they regularly use. Facebook is great for those who want to access smaller niche markets as well as international markets.

Instagram

The social network is extremely well-known and ranks second to Facebook. It's been operating for a while but has shown to be reliable and efficient over the course of. The biggest demographic of users on the platform is teenagers and millennials and the least popular is older people. But, globally, Instagram has a following quite similar to Facebook.

Instagram primarily relies on images and photos. It is a distinctive characteristic. In order to succeed with this site You must use quality images and photographs. It is also possible to make videos but text is not widely used in Instagram. It's almost exclusively mobile, which means that the majority of users are able to access the platform via mobile devices like tablets phones and computers.

This website is ideal to showcase artistic creations as well as any other products better displayed in photographs. People who provide certain services that are intangible like web design, for instance, may not find this platform beneficial. This website is perfect for marketing the international market, millennials and females. For most small companies is to create high-quality content especially photos and videos which appeal to the people who are here.

The target audience of Instagram is comprised of urban and suburban millennials, teens, young people and others. It also has of females and males using Instagram, making Instagram an excellent platform for targeting female followers and clients. As the site is mostly mobile, all the apps and tools are most commonly accessible on mobile devices. It is not possible to achieve much using the desktop platform, even while there are some application software to assist with this. These programs include Buffer along with Hoot Suite. They can assist you in taking photos or upload and edit the photos on your personal computer.

Based on the industry you are in, Instagram can be an great platform to promote your brand and products. Consider the products you sell and, whether they are attractive physically so you can capture photos and then share them with your followers on Instagram. If your job is creative like a shoe or clothing designer, chef, jeweler, others, Instagram is the perfect place to showcase your company.

In 2018, an average Instagram user uses around half an hour on the site every single day. With over 800 million active users per day, you are guaranteed an excellent chance of getting many followers, potential leads and possibly even brand new customers. Instagram allows you to share a picture along with 3-10 stories every day that highlight your business. There are various ways to bring fans, users and potential customers to your application make sure you discover more information about how to drive users to your Instagram account.

Twitter

The social media platform is ideal for certain businesses, but it's not the best for all. It is the reason you have be aware of the different types of types of social media. Twitter is great for small post and also linking to articles and blog posts. It is built for users to share brief messages, also known as tweets. You can, however, share images, links and videos, as well as polls and more.

Twitter is perfect for business who target tech-savvy customers and elites. They appreciate concise and precise communications as well as information that is snazzy in pieces. Be aware that this is the third biggest social media site, so being right here is an immense benefit. If you are a business owner it is recommended to set up your own Twitter account for your business and then begin communicating with customers as well as other users using the service. Once you have done this it, you'll get the attention of others and create a distinct brand.

Ideal posts to publish include announcements about business, launches and other events, timely updates or shout-outs. Also, you can follow other users' tweets. It is recommended to tweet anywhere between one and three every day, reaching over the 275 million monthly users.

To sign up for an account for yourself on Twitter just visit the Twitter for Business page and follow the steps to sign up. When your account is created and up, you'll need to begin following prominent names, notable people, and people in your field. Also, you should begin to post news and hyperlinks to helpful content as well as useful writing. Re-tweeting can be extremely beneficial, to re-tweet content you find fascinating, engaging or exciting and other such things. Be aware that there are consumers that rely on platforms like Twitter for communication with companies and get the best customer service.

If you're a highly well-known brand or don't own an online blog, then you might want to avoid this site. Be aware, however, that there are numerous businesses which benefit from this platform. The reason for this is their distinctive products and brands along with a distinct voice. Make sure you stand out in order to make yourself make yourself stand out from others. Companies benefit from Twitter by engaging with their clients and listen to them as they share their thoughts and voice their worries.

If you have the ability to produce interesting and engaging content, Twitter is a great way to get the message across to the public at large. There are tools available to aid you with this, like Hash-tags. The hashtag can increase the visibility of your blog and draw people's attention who may read and tweet your article. Through this social media platform, it is important to achieve a healthy an equilibrium. It is important to share your articles, content, and much more, however keep in mind to also share posts of other brands as well as your friends.

LinkedIn

Even though LinkedIn isn't necessarily the most viewed social media platform but it is still awash with an average of 260 million people every month. It's one of the most professional social networks and ideal for finding top talent and presenting your company and yourself as professional attire, trustworthy and capable of the job. That's why LinkedIn is considered to be the best social media website for business as well as professionals. Many users look to LinkedIn as their online resume.

Additionally, it is a platform that allows business-to-business interaction in which professionals get together and connect. The user base of this platform comprised of professional from various industries. It has approximately 5 million accounts active. If you are an account holder you should consider posting your content on the website between 1 and every 4 days. The content you post should be focused on business launches, product launches events, or any other interesting but relevant content, as well hyperlinks to other content on the web.

If you make use of this site properly, you'll be able to connect with the industry's top executives, draw clients, and increase sales. In the end, you could be a thought-leader and an acknowledged expert in your field. Once you're a highly respected authority in your field and you're certain to gain more followers, and certainly greater revenues.

It is advisable for any small company to set up a LinkedIn company page. It is an excellent platform for professional and business users as it will showcase your business to people who are relevant. Being on LinkedIn will also mean you've established a solid profile on a professional social networking site. Once your profile is created, share content to others and also posting relevant articles.

It is possible to use LinkedIn for a variety of other purposes including headhunting candidates and finding potential employees.

The majority of users make their profiles look like resumes, and companies make profiles to showcase their business. Make sure that you represent yourself in a way which reveals details about the culture of your company. Think about joining groups that are industry-related so that you are able to meet with businesses and experts in the same industry. In this way, you'll have the opportunity to respond to questions and provide solutions to ensure you can be acknowledged as an industry expert. This will bring in an increase in followers to your website and your business's Facebook page.

YouTube

Another popular social media website is the platform for sharing videos on YouTube. YouTube lets users upload, share, browse as well as comment and rate videos. It is owned by Google and is extremely popular among users across all over the world. The site has grown in popularity as a news site as well as entertainment, information and. YouTube's primary users are people who do general research as well as people who are looking for information as well as entertainment. Over three billion searches that are conducted through the site each month as well as 1.6 billion users active every month. With such a huge fan base that it is logical to create a YouTube page YouTube and to take advantage of the opportunity to market.

One of the best aspects of the website is the fact that users can share informative, imaginative as well as visual material. The power of creativity is what powers the site and keeps people returning time and time again. When you join the website and establishing your company page, it is recommended to create high-quality interesting, informative, and creative videos that make your point known and make it easier for followers to your page and, in a short period of time, your webpage will gain an impressive and sustained audience. It is recommended to upload approximately 1 to three videos per week in order to keep followers interested.

YouTube is the second-largest web search engine after Google and also the biggest streaming platform for video globally, YouTube provides businesses with the opportunity to connect to their customers. YouTube is particularly suited to firms that are able to use videos for reaching out to their customers and drive an issue home. If you're able to instruct to, inform, or educate by using videos, YouTube is the perfect option for your company. Imagine a landscaping firm who teaches viewers how to grow a particular plant or flower.

But, YouTube does require some work and effort compared to other social networks. As the site for sharing videos it is necessary spend the time, effort and know-how to make your own video. There is a chance that you require help in the beginning with your videos. If you're unable to produce quality content consider seeking help through a third party. Or, you might need to purchase a video editing software that will aid you in your creation of video content.

It is recommended to concentrate on creating between five and ten videos and then upload at minimum one per week. The length of videos varies between three and 10 minutes. It is not necessary to entertain, however they could be educational or informative. It appears that a large portion of the videos available on the site include animated explanations, interviews or how-to instructional videos.

Snapchat

One of the latest yet popular social media platforms is referred to as Snapchat. It is a visual platform whose content is limited in time. It is distinct from other social networks in this regard. The users and members of this application program share different content including photos and video to one another and occasionally post content to their social media accounts. The posts are only for 24 hours.

Snapchat is now a chat platform. You can Snapchat and communicate with friends, share photos as well as store them. It can as well share content from media and even events. The app is made to store published content for only 24 hours, you're capable of saving any images you love to your phone or another device. So, you are able to view videos via your Snapchat account, and later share it on different apps.

One benefit that this site has over other ones is that there's less pressure to create stunningly refined content. It is due to its nature of being temporary. It also lets you know who among your viewers viewed your posts. One of the most popular features on Snapchat is its Stories feature. The small company profile you have is likely to utilize the feature frequently. It is a challenge because the videos and other information you post are only accessible to people who are following your profile. So, you must focus on gaining followers to ensure that you've got the potential to reach a large audience with your material. Thanks to using the Stories feature, you're in a position to create high quality and engaging media.

Google My Business

This particular platform has been designed especially for businesses. Google My Business, therefore provides you with a place which allows you to display your services, business as well as your brand's image to customers. The most popular audience on Google My Business will be every Google person who is looking for local businesses for certain product or service.

In this website, you'll be required to build a complete and clear professional profile. A profile must be clear about your company's activities and the products or services you offer or the products you offer along with contacts. Google My Business receives monthly visitors of around 3.5 billion search results each every day. You do not have to post regularly on your website or make it available to others. It is important that users can find your company.

Google My Business is more than a directory for businesses. The service allows businesses to appear its location on Google Maps and also appear on local searches. Customers can review your company and provide reviews. A lot of people refer to this website as the biggest directory of businesses. This makes it logical to any company, big or small to be listed there and have a presence particularly if it has an physical address.

For your business to be included in the first place, you must make an account. It will be possible for clients to access all information regarding your company such as your business's name, address, and contact details, as well as the items that you provide or which you provide. When you declare your address, clients are able to find you on the web and make suggestions to fellow customers and discover specific characteristics which could draw them to your business.

It is essential that you have the most complete information you can in your profile. In particular, you have be sure to list your hours of opening and closing and photos of the building as well as a menu, listing of the products that are available for sale, etc. In essence, any company that is that is listed in Google My Business will outrank the other companies that are not on the list.

It is due to the local pack, which is an essential part of all businesses' search results through Google. If you are a small-scale business owner particularly one that has an online presence it will be a huge benefit from having a profile for your business with such a reputable platform. It is easy to create a profile to do, quick and requires only a few minutes. Since Google as the biggest search engine it is likely that your business can greatly benefit from having being listed here.

Chapter 11: Marketing And Advertising

Most people think that advertising and marketing mean the same and identical things. Many marketers think there's only a thin separation between them. The truth is that they're distinct despite sharing the same goals. It is the intention to inform consumers about products and services. merchandise that are offered for sale.

Although both advertising and marketing are remarkably similar however, they do have some significant distinctions. Businesses as well as their managers and owners to understand the distinctions and similarities to plan strategies to increase sales and improve customer acquisition.

The difference between advertising and Marketing

It's not surprising that there's confusion over the difference between advertising and marketing. They're very distinct, even when they are attempting to connect with consumers through promotion of products and services. If you are able to distinguish between them and carry out your market research correctly to have the ability to set your company on the path to success.

Marketing

Marketing is an extensive process of the creation of ideas, designing or brainstorming, planning analysis, and strategizing on how to connect a product or service to a particular audience in the most efficient way.

Marketing is the process of planning, coordinating and execution of various initiatives aimed at connecting buyers and sellers to facilitate the benefit of both the purchase and sale of services and products.

Step-by-step procedure

Marketing can be thought of as a process that is step-by-step. The process starts with an encapsulated selling point which is a short yet compelling phrase that establishes the business.

The concept or message that will serve as the primary concept that guides the efforts you make to find potential customers who might be curious about what you're offering.

Analysis and research

Marketing requires the process of research and analysis. This involves studying your prospective market, and then creating design and terminology that can ultimately affect the marketplace. The key is create missions statements and slogans that convey the message you want to convey. They are crucial for your marketing plan overall. We can divide the strategy into four distinct elements. They are also known as the 4Ps, and comprise of product, place pricing, promotion and price.

Marketing campaigns convey an advertisement that let the general public know who may make use of the product, as well as any other pertinent details. The marketing materials used in the campaign convey this message, that in turn establishes the character and tone of the brand and product. The other aspects are distribution and price of the item.

The pie of marketing is viewed as an artifact

Marketing is also viewed as a piece of pie cut into slices. The slices can be represented through marketing research, advertising as well as media planning, public relations as well as marketing strategy, community relations as well as customer service. We can conclude that advertising, though well-known and efficient but it is only one part of marketing.

Although all aspects of marketing are independent but they must be in sync to accomplish what is the business's goal. Marketing is an exhausting one. It requires a lot of time and time to research in order to successfully run a campaign for marketing. It is easy to define marketing as everything that a company does to make it easier for customers to exchange information or deal with its customers.

Before you can run any type of advertisement or promotion you must do market research to identify who your people are. Following the market research, you might discover that social media can be a better platform to place advertisements than buying spaces on printed or electronic media.

Sometimes the situation could be writing an opinion piece for local newspapers or magazines can yield far superior outcomes. Thus, when the market research has been completed It is time to design a suitable marketIng strategy and begin to communicate your customers and clients using the most effective method.

Advertising

Advertising can be described as basically the act of spreading the word regarding the product or service in order to make it known by a particular crowd. In this manner the use of a description to explain the concept of the service or product to the general public.

Advertising includes campaigns on digital and print media, and recently, on digital media. The advertising campaign should include imaginative content as well as positioning within the media chosen. It is vital that an advert is placed at timing

Advertising definition

Every advertisement is a publicly commercial announcement, which is paid for and contains an appealing message that is sent by an individual or a company for customers that are prospective or already in the market.

Like we said earlier, marketing is only an aspect of the marketing procedure in general. It's, in actual it is the only element of marketing which involves making sure that the world gets to know more about your company and its products, services and your brand. Nearly all advertisements are branded with the sponsor's name and the name of the brand.

Advertising includes placing advertisements in various media, including television and billboards. Direct mail magazine, billboards and newspapers and online. It's crucial to understand that the printing media is rapidly disappearing and advertisers are looking for different avenues in which to put their advertisements. They are looking for unusual spots including the tops of taxis, in wall surfaces, at bus stops and more.

Advertising's primary goal is to communicate the message to consumers. It involves many steps that include creating advertisements that align with the needs and desires of customers who are interested in purchasing. A successful campaign makes the use of various mediums to create the right atmosphere and create excitement regarding the product or service which are advertised.

The various media options are based on the target group of people. Particularly for young people like teens and young people the social media websites work best for ads spots.

Other people, like those who are retired, television and radio could be a good option. Others consumer groups could be more effectively reached through billboards, newspapers and magazines' advertisements. However, even then, you're likely to discover that many advertisements employ multiple medium in order to reach the largest potential audience.

How do you promote

Advertising is the method to communicate to customers and the general population about the services or products. Advertising is the process of conceiving programs that connect a company's offerings and services to the desires and needs of the general public. The main feature of an campaign to promote itself is the use of various different media, in order to communicate a message and also create a anticipation and buzz around an item or product or.